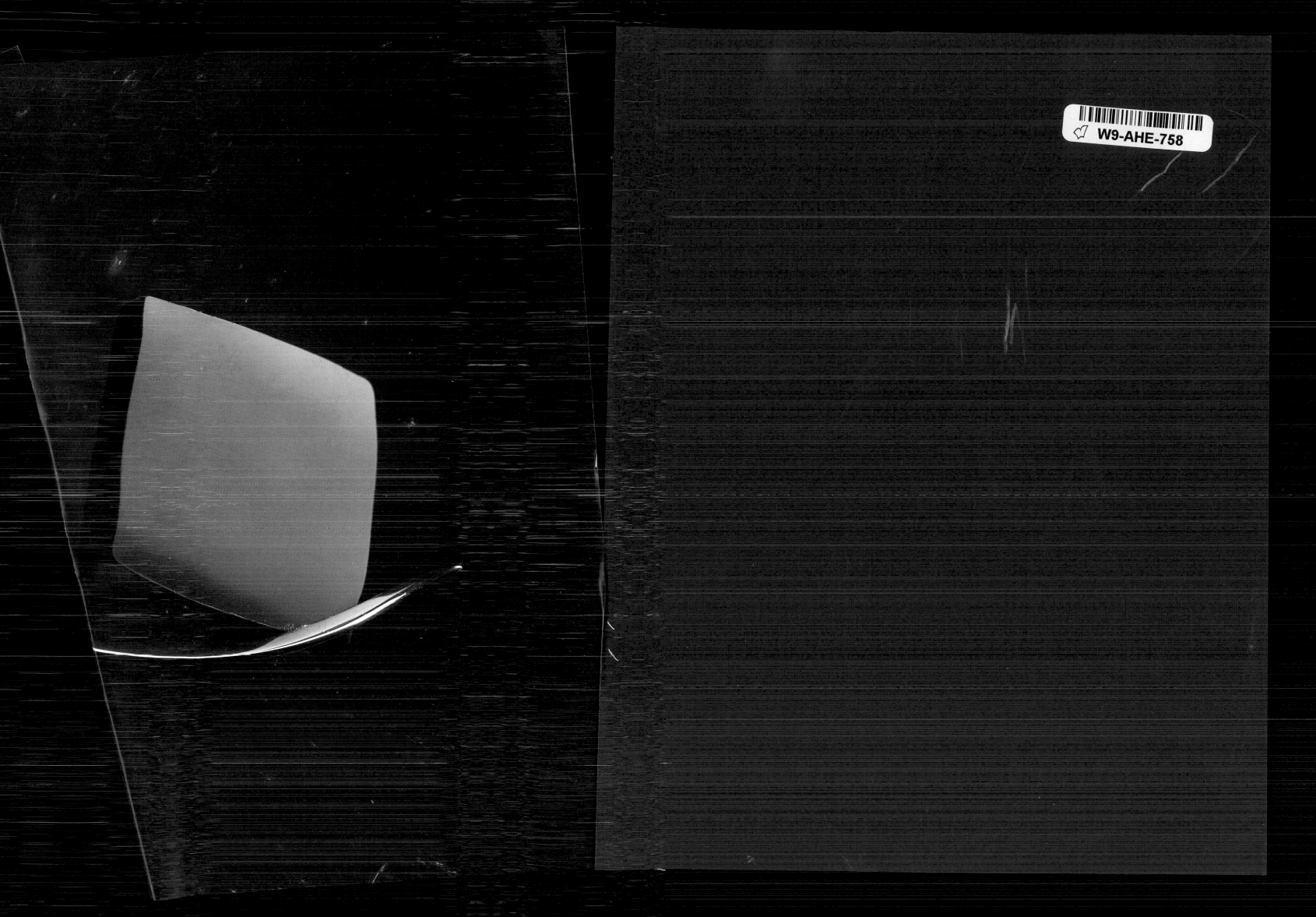

W9-AHE-758

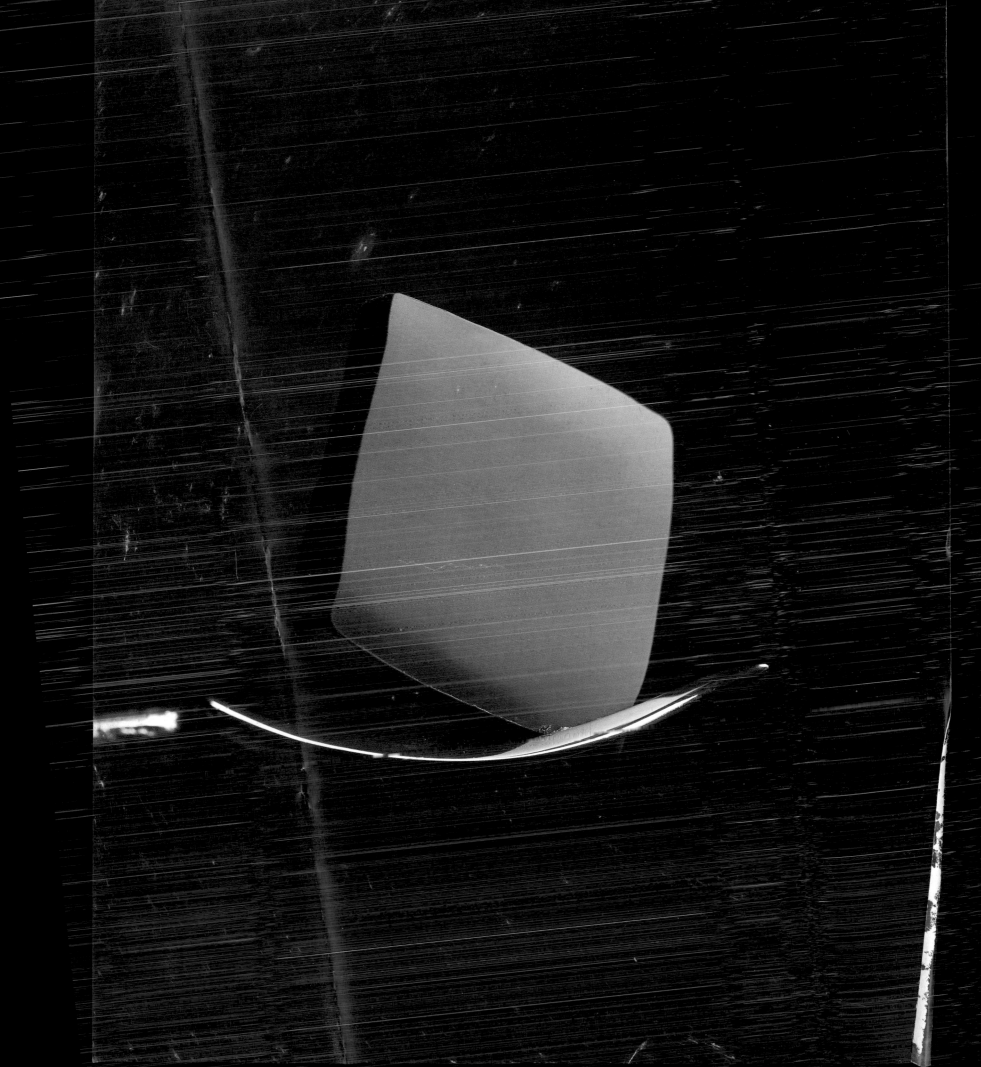

Additional text: Michele Carles

Photographs: Christine Fleurent

La Maison du Chocolat

Transcendent Desserts by the Legendary Chocolatier

Robert Linxe

RIZZOLI
NEW YORK

contents

Left: Tamanoco,
a box of five different
plain ganache
chocolates, made from
different types of
cocoa.

"A successful ganache blend allows each individual

cocoa flavor to stand out. Each cocoa bean has

a taste that is truly unique, a personality as distinct

as the sound made by a musical instrument, or the

voice of an opera singer."

Robert Linxe

Left: Rigoletto,
a subtle mixture
of milk chocolate
and caramel.
Below: Jolika,
a pistacho-flavored
marzipan coated in
bittersweet chocolate.

Right: Cocoa Powder from La Maison du Chocolat.
Below: Habanera, a gift box composed of two fruit-scented ganache-filled chocolates: peach and plum.

Chocolate comes in many forms—bars, truffles, powder, candies—and can also become cakes, beverages, mousses, soufflés, ice cream….This characteristic, whether magic or divine, explains why chocolate arouses such passion. It is the reason why Carl von Linné classified chocolate as *theobroma*, "food of the gods," and why Robert Linxe built his temple: La Maison du Chocolat (The House of Chocolate). It is no small coincidence, perhaps, that the Swedish botanist and Basque chocolate-maker share the initial syllable of their last name. There are other similarities: The Scientist and the Artisan share a mutual concern for perfection, for quality, for discipline, and a constant craving that fuels their curiosity and incites them to search ever deeper. "I may be considered an artist," says Linxe, "but I am first and foremost a craftsman. Every gesture is an act of skill, based on years of experience, which must be conveyed."

"You can never achieve perfection," says the founder of La Maison du Chocolat. "It takes stubbornness, perseverance, and a lot, a lot of hard work, to get…somewhere. You must taste, discern, and evaluate. But this 'somewhere,' for me, is still out of reach. Even though I have not yet attained it, I am content with what I have done. Creation is a never-ending process, constantly improving upon itself."

Chocolate-Lover and Musician

It was 1955 when the young Robert Linxe opened La Marquise de Presles in Paris; a sort of prelude to his grand overture in chocolate that was to follow. His range of candies was based on Swiss chocolate-making traditions, where he learned his craft. It was there, too, that he learned to be meticulous, amongst other skills of the trade.

1953   Following a chocolate-making course in Switzerland, Robert Linxe starts a two-year apprenticeship at

a Parisian restaurant.

1955   The 25-year-old Linxe buys the premises of a former chocolate-pastry shop on the rue de Presles in Paris,

called La Marquise de Presles.

1977   The first *Maison du Chocolat* is opened at 255, rue du Faubourg-Saint-Honore.

1987   The second store opens at 52 rue Francois 1er, followed by another store two years later at 8, boulevard

de la Madeleine.

1990   La Maison du Chocolat opens in New York.

1992   Linxe appears on the prestigious French television talk show, *Bouillon de Culture*.

1995   Two more stores open in Paris: 19, rue de Sevres and 89, avenue Raymond-Poincaré.

1997   A special gift box is created in honor of the 20th anniversary of La Maison du Chocolat.

1998   La Maison du Chocolat opens in Tokyo.

2000   Another store in New York opens at Rockefeller Center; membership in the Comité Colbert, one of the highest

honors in the French luxury goods industry.

Twenty years later, this pioneer opened the first Maison du Chocolat, on the rue Faubourg Saint-Honoré, almost directly opposite the celebrated music hall, La Salle Pleyel. This was an incredible omen for such an enthusiastic music-lover. It provided a steady flow of like-minded clientele, musically inclined and passionate about chocolate, and it also provided the name of one of his most well-known cakes.

When Linxe founded La Maison du Chocolat, he chose for his logo the *metate,* a tool with indisputable historic significance. It was an Indian implement, slightly curved and made from stone, which was used to crush cocoa beans, along with a *metlapilli,* a stone roller.

Left: Coco, a milk chocolate ganache flavored with coconut and rum beneath a dark chocolate coating, decorated with grated coconut. This page: Petits carrés (little squares) of dark and milk chocolate.

The Finest Beans

But how is a chocolate born? For the "composer" Linxe, always halfway between tradition and innovation, there are no rules. "Above all, it is a question of instincts, and spontaneity. It begins with the inspiration—a place, a piece of music, an aroma, a conversation, an association and suddenly the idea is there, and the mixture becomes obvious. This is where the craft begins: trials and sample testing until the balance of flavor and texture is achieved. Tasting, tasting, and tasting, until the blend is just right, with each flavor highlighting the other in perfect harmony. It is a delicate balance, comparable to 'carving out' a melody." Musical metaphor is a constant theme.

Chocolate milk to drink
hot or cold.

To create the perfect chocolate, Linxe has become a master of his craft. His skill and talent are omnipresent, and the key to his success is constant testing of all ingredients. This begins with the cocoa beans, which he likens to musical notes, or instruments in an orchestra. Each type of bean is chosen for a specific purpose, based on its origins and grower. Much like grapes destined for wine, the characteristics and quality of a candy will be directly related to the type and origin of the cocoa beans, where the beans were grown, and also how the different bean types are blended. Each bite of a Linxe chocolate is like a voyage through one the many different cocoa tastes of the world.

Most chocolate aficionados agree that the finest beans come from South and Central America, which is historically accurate, but there are also quality cocoa plantations in Madagascar, Java, and Ceylon, to name but a few. This vast palate of international flavors leaves the chocolate artisan with quite a selection from which to make his blends. Over time, La Maison du Chocolat has developed a preference for certain types of beans, notably those from Venezuela, Ecuador, Ghana, and Indonesia. Linxe and his team are still searching out new beans, constantly tasting and testing, and creating and inventing new taste combinations and flavorings to tantalize the tastebuds of chocolate lovers everywhere.

The same rigorous selection is applied to the ingredients that make up the flavor blends: The finest lemons from southern Spain, fresh mint grown in Morocco, and so on. Linxe uses only the best ingredients from around the world, and has conveyed his preferences to his international team of expert chocolate makers. They have also been taught to use these ingredients with the same respect and attention to detail, resulting in the finest chocolates each and every time.

Bacchus, a creamy
ganache with rum-soaked
raisins or currants.

Cocoa Bean Types

The following are the three main types of cocoa trees:

- *Criollo*: One of the oldest types, but also the most delicate and rare (it has very low yields); beans make an exceptionally delicate chocolate.

- *Forastero*: Native to the upper Amazon but transplanted to Africa, mainly the Ivory Coast. Very hardy, with high yields, these beans are full-flavored and robust—the "robusta" of cocoa trees.

- *Trinitario*: A cross between Criollo and Forastero. Grown primarily in the Americas, Indonesia, and Sri Lanka. This gets its strength from Forastero and subtlety from Criollo, which allows for a vast range of flavors.

Where a bean is grown, as opposed to the type, will have the most influence on its flavor, which we call its "character." Beans from Venezuela are sought after for their perfectly balanced aroma; cocoa from Guayaquil, in Ecuador, is noted for its strength; beans from Martinique are pungent and slightly smoky; beans from Brazil tend to have a high cocoa fat content, and are perfect for blending. Madagascar produces cocoa that is very strong and dominant, while Ceylonese and Indonesian beans are noted more for the aromatic scent than their powerful taste. These are the ideal partner for more robust beans. Caribbean cocoa is full-bodied and aromatic; Arriba, from Trinidad is slightly bitter but perfect for blends and couverture—a large bar of chocolate. Sumatran beans are cultivated on hot, humid hillsides, making them acidic. African beans (Ghana, Togo, Ivory Coast) are sought after for their sharp, strong, intense flavor.

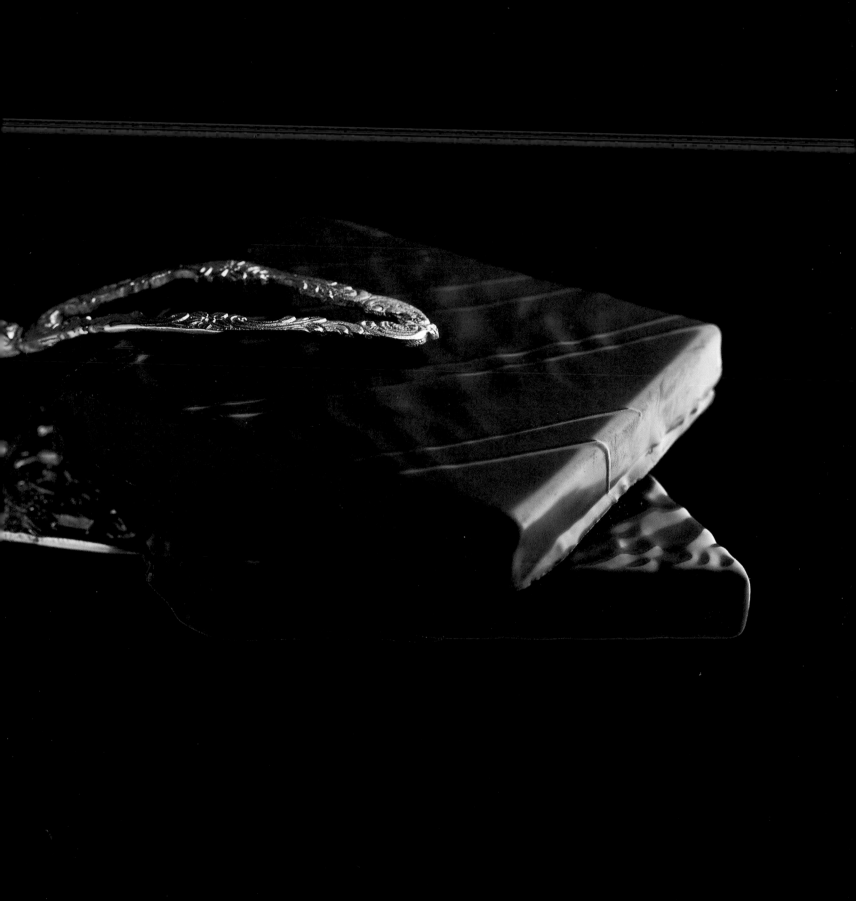

"Blending a chocolate is just like making a perfume—

seeking the balance is everything. In fact, I have even

made perfumes with a hint of cocoa in them. And,

like the chocolate-maker, the art of the perfume-

maker is entirely manual: I'm not a chemist, I'm

more like a cook, experimenting with flavors and

mixtures....

And if you close your eyes, what trace does

a woman leave? A scent, a taste...."

Jean-Paul Guerlain

Left: Guayaquil, a slightly vanilla-scented ganache, and Bresilien, a coffee ganache beneath a full-flavored coating.

Easter creations
from La Maison
du Chocolat.
Right: A dark
chocolate, made from
a blend of Orinoco
and Maracaïbo.

The "Sorcerer of Ganache"

Robert Linxe has been affectionately nicknamed the "Sorcerer of Ganache" but his attention to detail does not stop with the insides of his candies. The coating is equally as important, and for his "couverture," he uses one of the finest chocolate brands in the world, Valrhona, to assemble his blends. A couverture, in chocolatier terms, is a huge bar of chocolate (6-10 pounds), made from ground cocoa beans, cocoa butter, and sugar. Linxe, and his closest associate, Pascal Le Gac, are most attentive to this phase of the chocolate-making process. A quality couverture can only be obtained from a mix of diverse, high-quality beans. Again, the origin of the beans and the production methods used in growing are key to the final taste; for example, South American beans tend to be slightly bitter, while those from Africa are fruity. The balance of flavors within the couverture must be precise, especially if it will later be used to coat a ganache that is a precise blend of flavors. For example, a chocolate-lemon filling requires a full-flavored coating while a honey-scented ganache needs a slightly acidic couverture. It is this precise blending, and layering of tastes and aromas that give each candy its personality.

A Never-Ending Symphony

The most crucial, but rewarding, part of the chocolate-making process remains the ganache interior. A ganache is simply a mixture of chocolate and cream, either on its own, or infused with another aroma. A truly great ganache is "the expression of all the cocoa beans that are used in a blend, each stamped with the personality and characteristics of its country of origin," says Linxe. He continues with his musical metaphor: "Like a melody, each candy should come to its fruition with the first bite, exploding on the palate and liberating its delicious tones, yet not detracting from the final chord that lingers after the candy is gone."

Left: The Flamenco gift
box contains two
flavors: dark chocolate
jasmin-basil ganache,
and milk chocolate
rosemary ganache.

On the surface, making ganache may seem like nothing more than chopping chocolate, boiling cream, and mixing the two. Child's play perhaps, but not if the result is to be up to Linxe's standards. "A ganache must be meltingly light, but still creamy and dense. The texture must be perfectly smooth, without a trace of coarseness to trip up the tongue, or compete with the delightful "crack" as the teeth break the crisp couverture coating."

To achieve such a pinnacle of gustatory satisfaction, a love of chocolate is not enough. It must be partnered with a lifetime of experience, and the skills accumulated through trial and error along the way.

"Creating a new recipe," confides Linxe, "is like an adventure: dangerous, yet always exciting. And the process cannot be hurried." The ideas usually come in an instant, but the final composition of a candy can take months. Often, cakes and pastries inspire taste combinations. For example, *Bacchus* existed as a candy, which later inspired the cake. *Andalousie* was born of a partnership between chocolate and lemon, and the name was given to both the candy and the cake. Likewise, the boundaries between "chocolatier" and "chocolate pastry chef" intermingle. The ingredient, chocolate, is so diverse (as this book demonstrates) that it inspires creation of all sorts. What must be shared is technique, and precision when creating and executing the craft.

This page: For Easter,
an egg-shaped,
caramel-colored box
filled with mixed
ganaches and
chocolate eggs.

Linxe's first creations were made in a laboratory, beneath his Maison du Chocolat store, and they were an overnight success. Rave reviews came pouring in from all parts, including a major French newspaper, which called Robert Linxe the "genie of the chocolate bar, sorcerer of the truffle, and magician of ganache, who works with the precision of a Swiss clockmaker…." Despite the praise, Linxe is never satisfied, and therein lies the key to his success. The desire for perfection, and an insatiable curiosity, push him ever onwards. Even when a

candy is successful, he still has questions. How it will be perceived over time? Will the pairing of tastes and aromas stay true? What other recipes must be created to carry on this passion, so delicate and fragile? The answer is that Robert Linxe *is* writing the never-ending symphony, so the questions will always be there. They are vital to the creative process, and no success is ever final.

Know Your Craft, Listen to Your Tastebuds

Alongside the skill of creating a sensation for the palate, the art of chocolate-making must also be a feast for the eyes. Linxe proudly describes a display of his creations, "Look at the different shapes and colors. There are squares, diamonds, and circles, all identifiable by their markings—stripes, criss-crosses—and their color, ranging from a pale chamois to mahogany and deep brown-black, or their coating, sometimes matte, sometimes glossy. The exterior is the first point of contact so it must be silky smooth and alluring to the eye and to the touch. It must be strong enough to contain the feast within, but not so thick as to overpower the luscious, tender ganache filling. It is the starting point for an exhilarating explosion of sensations and tastes.

Naming a chocolate candy is very different from naming and fant. Right from the outset, it has a discernible character and personality, which must be captured in a single word.

Left: Shaped like the outer shell of a chestnut, this coating contains finely ground chestnuts scented with rum and a hint of vanilla.
This page: Valencia, a whipped ganache scented with orange liqueur.

21

"Jewelers and chocolate makers have a great deal in common. Whether we work with precious gemstones or cocoa beans, we are always seeking out the most beautiful, the rarest, the most exceptional. Our job is to mold, transform, and invent when creating a unique piece of jewelery or candy. Balance, form, and color are of prime importance. We also share a tradition of craftsmanship and work based on precision, emotion, and passion."

Alain Boucheron, jeweler

Three plain ganache chocolates, a tempting introduction. Bohême is a gentle milk chocolate, Quito is a scintillating yet subtle ganache, and Caracas is a powerful cocoa ganache.

"Just like writing a musical score," says Linxe, "combining the flavors of different cocoa beans is an art. When successful, it releases the full range of aromas and taste sensations."

As La Maison du Chocolat continues to evolve towards the future, it carries with it this same spirit of creativity and curiosity that founded its success. It remains the fruit of all its labor, and stamped with the inimitable personality of its founder. Fired by a passion for chocolate, blended with a love of music, it is built upon a foundation of refinement and exquisitely good taste.

These efforts were rewarded in the year 2000, when La Maison du Chocolat was admitted to the prestigious Comité Colbert, a body comprised of top French luxury goods companies and organizations, dedicated to quality and excellence, and the preservation of French culture and innovation.

Michèle Carles

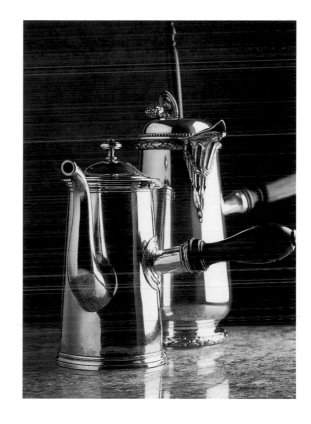

Above: Sterling silver hot cocoa servers. Left: Minerva, a dark chocolate praline exploding with the flavors of orange peel, rum-soaked raisins, walnuts, and pistachios.

La Maison du Chocolat
offers a rainbow of
chocolate bars,
ranging from Cuana
made from 73% cocoa,
to milk chocolate
Merida and white
chocolate Tolima.

Chocolate bars from La Maison du Chocolat

For each recipe, we recommend a specific type of chocolate in the ingredient list. These blends are specially made for La Maison du Chocolat and only available in our stores. The recipes can be made with other chocolate brands, but the results will not be authentically Maison du Chocolat.

Coro   100% cocoa, without any added sugar. This high-quality chocolate is as pure as they come, bursting with cocoa flavor. Use only in very small quantities.

Cuana   73% cocoa. A powerful chocolate, available in very thin bars to best appreciate its full-flavor. This goes well with more subtle chocolate bars.

Orinoco   65% cocoa. This is the chocolate lovers' chocolate. Powerful and well balanced, this is ideal for pairing with any chocolate, especially Maracaïbo.

Ordinary   62% cocoa. This is the most versatile blend for baking. It can be used on its own, or with Maracaïbo.

Maracaïbo   57% cocoa. A refined and delicate chocolate.

Merida   35% cocoa. This is authentic milk chocolate, perfectly balanced and not too sweet.

Perfect partners:
Dark chocolate peach
ganache and
milk chocolate plum
ganache.

Cookies, Candies, and Other Sweet Things

Makes about 45-50 chocolates
Preparation: 15 minutes
Cooking time: about 3 minutes

Cherry Chocolates

Caissettes aux griottes

1 pound bittersweet chocolate
(ordinary bittersweet)
³/₄ cup heavy cream
1 vanilla bean
3 tablespoons unsalted butter
6 tablespoons kirsch
2 ounces cherries
(preferably sour cherries), pitted
About 25 small paper candy cases

1. Place the chocolate on a chopping block and chop finely with a knife. Put in a heatproof mixing bowl. Set aside.

2. Pour the heavy cream into a saucepan and set aside. With a small knife, split the vanilla bean lengthwise down the middle and scrape out the little black seeds. Place the vanilla seeds and bean in the cream, then bring to a boil.
As soon as the cream boils, remove from the heat, wait 20 seconds, stir, then pour over the chopped chocolate. Let stand for a few seconds, then remove the vanilla bean. Whisk to combine in a circular motion, starting from the middle and working out.

3. As soon as the chocolate is completely melted and the mixture is homogenous, stir in the butter. Mix for a few seconds, then add the kirsch and stir to blend. Refrigerate for 4 hours.

4. To assemble: Finely chop the cherries and set aside. Return the chocolate mixture to the top of a double boiler set over low heat to soften. Off the heat, beat with a mixer until smooth and creamy.

5. Transfer to a pastry bag fitted with a small star tip. Pipe into the paper case, filling about three-quarters full. Sprinkle chopped cherries over each and then cover with a final rosette of piped chocolate. Set aside to harden before serving.

Tip: Choose cream with a fat content of about 30-35% for a lighter result.

Macarons au chocolat

Chocolate-Almond Macarons

1 ½ cups plus 1 tablespoon
ground almonds

2 ½ tablespoons unsweetened
cocoa powder

3 cups confectioners' sugar

5 egg whites

For the chocolate ganache

14 ounces bittersweet chocolate

(9 ounces orinoco,

5 ounces maracaïbo)

1 cup heavy cream

1. Preheat the oven to 350°.
Line a baking sheet with
parchment paper. Sift together
the ground almonds, cocoa
powder, and 2 ½ cups of the
sugar into a large bowl.
Set aside.

2. Place the egg whites in
another large mixing bowl and
beat until they hold firm peaks.
Add the remaining sugar and
beat until stiff. With a spatula,
gently fold in the ground
almond mixture, folding just
until the batter is smooth and
light.

3. Transfer the almond mixture
to a pastry bag fitted with a
round tip. Pipe 40 small round
mounds onto the prepared
sheet.

4. Bake for 20 minutes.
Remove from the oven. Lightly
moisten the parchment paper
with a pastry brush dipped in
water, and then remove the
macarons. Set aside to cool.

5. Meanwhile, prepare the
chocolate ganache: Chop the
chocolate and place in a
heatproof bowl. Place the heavy
cream in a saucepan and bring
to a boil. Pour the boiling cream
over the chocolate and let melt.
Stir to blend, then set aside to
let the ganache harden slightly.

6. To assemble: Spread the flat
side of one macaron with the
ganache and sandwich with
another macaron, flat-sides
together. Repeat for the
remaining macarons.

Tip: For successful beaten egg
whites, avoid getting yolk mixed
into the whites, and add a pinch
of salt just before beating.

Chocolate-Coffee

Roméo

Beneath a dark chocolate exterior, lies a
perfect match: light and fluffy milk chocolate
buttercream infused with robust, freshly
ground mocha. This meeting of tastes is as
inevitable as that of Shakespeare's star-
crossed lovers. No doubt, their legendary
image has inspired countless others—Berlioz,
Gounod—but here, the result is a candy that
is subtle, smooth, and irresistible.

Tuiles a l'orange et aux amandes

Orange-Almond Tile Cookies

7 tablespoons unsalted butter

2 unwaxed oranges, organic if possible

$1/3$ cup all-purpose flour

$3/4$ cup granulated sugar

Heaping $1/2$ cup sliced almonds

1. Prepare the clarified butter: Melt the butter and set aside to cool slightly. With a spoon, remove the top (clear) layer of the melted butter and place in another small dish. Discard the milky solids that sink to the bottom of the pan.

2. Preheat the oven to 350°. Grease a baking sheet. Remove the orange zest with a knife or vegetable peeler. Slice the zest into long, thin strips and set aside. Squeeze the juice from the oranges and strain. Reserve a scant 3 tablespoons.

3. Place the orange zest in a mixing bowl. Add the flour, sugar, clarified butter, orange juice, and stir well. Stir in the sliced almonds.

4. Transfer a soupspoon of batter to the prepared tray. Spread to obtain a thin 2 $1/2$-inch circle. Repeat 5 more times.

5. Bake until just golden, about 10 minutes. Meanwhile, prepare a clean rolling pin.

6. Remove the baking sheet from the oven. Wait a few seconds, then remove the cookies with a rubber spatula and transfer immediately to the rolling pin to shape them. Remove when cool and hard. Continue baking in small batches until the batter is finished.

Tip: You can serve these cookies with chocolate cream, sorbet, or ice cream.

Makes about 20 cookies
Preparation: 15 minutes
Cooking time: about 25 minutes

Florentins

Chocolate Fruit and Nut Cookies

1 ¹/₂ cups candied orange peel

1 cup mixed candied fruit

3 ¹/₂ cups sliced almonds

¹/₂ cup all-purpose flour

7 tablespoons honey

1 ¹/₂ cups granulated sugar

8 tablespoons unsalted butter

6 tablespoons heavy cream

For the chocolate coating

12 ounces bittersweet chocolate

(6 ounces orinoco, 6 ounces ordinary)

1. One day before serving: Line a large baking sheet with parchment paper. With a sharp knife, chop the orange peel and candied fruit into very small pieces. In a large mixing bowl, combine the chopped orange peel, candied fruit, sliced almonds, and flour and mix well.

2. In a saucepan, combine the honey, sugar, butter, and cream and bring to a boil. Cook over medium heat for 10 minutes, whisking occasionally.

3. Remove from the heat and gently fold in the orange peel mixture. Pour onto the prepared baking sheet and spread evenly. Refrigerate for at least 12 hours.

4. The next day: Preheat the oven to 350°. Using a soup spoon, scoop out a spoonful of the batter and roll into a ball shape. Spread in the center of a 4-inch nonstick tart pan to form a circle. Repeat for the remaining batter. (You could also place the spoonfuls of batter directly onto a baking sheet, spreading the circles about ¹/₄-inch thick.)

5. Bake for 10-12 minutes, until golden brown. Remove from the oven and transfer cookies to a sheet of parchment paper placed on top of a cooling rack (to keep them flat) and set aside to cool.

6. Prepare the chocolate coating: See the recipe for Tempering Chocolate (page 164). When the chocolate is melted and still warm (but not boiling), spread an even layer over the smooth side of the cookies, chill for 3 minutes, then remove from the refrigerator and set aside to harden. If desired, before the chocolate sets completely, make a wavy pattern in the chocolate using the tines of a fork.

Tip: The cookies will keep in an airtight container for about 10 days. If the weather is very humid, bake the cookies for several more minutes.

Chocolate-Mint

Zagora

Beneath a coating of bittersweet chocolate,
a mint-scented ganache. The freshest of mint
leaves are snipped with a scissors to release a
maximum of flavor before being infused in
the cream. The resulting taste is fresh and
delicate, but powerful.

The name comes from a southern
Moroccan village, which is home to the finest
mint tea in the world.

Makes about 1 ¼ pounds
Preparation: 10 minutes
Cooking time: 20 minutes

Bittersweet Chexolate-Nut Candy

1. Preheat the oven to 325°. Combine the almonds, pistachios, and hazelnuts in a baking dish. Place in the oven to brown for about 6 minutes. Remove from the oven and set aside. Lower the heat to 100°. Place the raisins and orange peel in an ovenproof dish and bake for 15 minutes, leaving the oven door slightly ajar.

2. Meanwhile, prepare the chocolate coating: See the recipe for Tempering Chocolate (page 164).

3. Place a large sheet of parchment paper on the counter. Add the warm (not hot) fruit and nuts to the melted chocolate. Stir to blend, then pour onto the parchment paper and spread to a thickness of about ½-inch with a spatula. Leave to harden in a cool place.

4. To serve, break into large pieces.

Tip: This candy will keep for 2 weeks in an airtight container.

Milk Chocolate Mendiants

Variation

Replace the bittersweet chocolate with high-quality milk chocolate (merida); the method and other quantities remain the same.

⅓ cup raisins
¼ cup candied orange peel, chopped into small cubes
3 tablespoons whole pistachios
¾ cup whole almonds
¾ cup whole hazelnuts

For the chocolate coating
12 ounces bittersweet chocolate (ordinary)

Makes about 70-80 truffles
Preparation: about 30 minutes
Cooking time: 5 minutes

Plain Truffles

1 pound bittersweet chocolate
(³/₄ pound ordinary, ¹/₄ pound cuana)
1 cup heavy cream
1 vanilla bean

For the coating
12 ounces bittersweet chocolate
(maracaïbo)
1 ¹/₂ cups unsweetened cocoa powder

1. Place the chocolate on a chopping block and chop finely with a knife. Put in a heatproof mixing bowl. Set aside.

2. Pour the heavy cream into a saucepan and set aside. With a small knife, split the vanilla bean lengthwise down the middle and scrape out the little black seeds. Place the vanilla seeds and bean in the cream, then bring to a boil. As soon as the cream boils, remove from the heat, wait 20 seconds, stir, then pour through a strainer into the chopped chocolate. Remove the vanilla bean.

3. Let stand for a few seconds. Whisk to combine in a circular motion, starting from the middle and working out. Whisk gently and stop as soon as the mixture is blended.

4. Set aside to cool (do not refrigerate). As soon as the truffle mixture is firm, set the bowl on top of a saucepan of gently simmering water just to warm through. Remove the bowl from the heat and whisk the chocolate mixture until smooth and creamy.

5. Cover a large baking sheet with aluminium foil or parchment paper. Transfer the chocolate mixture to a large pastry bag fitted with a large plain tip. Pipe out walnut-sized balls onto the prepared tray and refrigerate to harden for at least 1 hour.

6. Meanwhile, prepare the coating: Break the chocolate into pieces and melt over a double boiler. Place the cocoa powder in a shallow dish.

7. When the truffles are hard, remove them from the refrigerator. Working a few at a time, dip the truffles into the melted chocolate, then remove with the help of a fork. Transfer immediately to the cocoa powder, roll around to coat completely, then remove to a sieve and shake off the excess. Set aside to harden. Repeat for the remaining truffles.

Tip: The sign of a very good truffle is the thinnest possible coating of cocoa powder on the outside.

Variations

Rum Truffles

Prepare in exactly the same manner, but add ¼ cup rum to the truffle mixture just before piping.

Cinnamon Truffles

Add 2-3 cinnamon sticks to the cream at the same time as the vanilla bean and remove at the same time. The rest of the preparation is the same.

Ginger Truffles

Peel a small piece of ginger (about 1 ounce) and cut into pieces. Place in the boiling cream and let infuse for 5 minutes. Pour the cream through a strainer onto the chopped chocolate to remove the ginger pieces. The rest of the preparation is the same.

Tea Truffles

Add ¼ cup leaf tea to the boiled cream and let infuse for 8 minutes. Pour the cream through a strainer onto the chopped chocolate to remove the tea. For a more interesting tea flavor, use two different types of tea; for example, half Lapsang Souchong and half Earl Grey.

Makes 70-80 truffles
Preparation: about 30 minutes
Cooking time: 5 minutes

Mint Truffles

Truffes à la menthe

1 pound bittersweet chocolate
(½ ordinary, ½ maracaïbo)
⅔ cup fresh mint leaves
1 cup heavy cream

For the coating
12 ounces bittersweet chocolate
(8 ounces maracaïbo,
4 ounces orinoco)
1 ½ cups unsweetened cocoa powder

1. Place the chocolate on a work surface and chop finely with a sharp knife. Transfer to a large heatproof bowl. Snip the mint leaves with scissors.

2. Place the cream in a saucepan and bring to a boil. Remove from the heat. Add the mint, cover, and leave to infuse for 8 minutes.

3. Strain the mint cream into the bowl of chopped chocolate. Let stand for several seconds. Blend with a whisk, using slow circular motions from the center to the edge of the bowl. When thoroughly combined, set aside to harden; do not refrigerate.

4. Place a large sheet of aluminum foil or parchment paper on the counter.

5. Transfer the chocolate to the top of a double boiler and warm gently over low heat. Whisk and remove from the heat. When the chocolate mixture is soft enough to pipe, transfer to a piping bag fitted with a large round tip. Pipe walnut-sized circles onto the foil or parchment paper. Refrigerate the truffles for at least 1 hour. Remove as soon as they are firm.

6. Prepare the coating: Place the cocoa powder in a shallow dish. Break the chocolate into pieces and place in the top of a double boiler to melt. As soon as the chocolate has melted, it is ready to use.

7. Dip the truffles into the melted chocolate and remove with a fork. Quickly transfer the wet truffles to the cocoa powder and roll to coat evenly. Transfer immediately to a sieve and shake off the excess cocoa powder. Set aside to harden.

Tip: Use ordinary fresh mint and be sure to use scissors, not a knife, to release all of the flavor.

Chocolate-Ginger

Maïko

Beneath a coating of bittersweet chocolate, a ginger-scented ganache. Fresh gingerroot is peeled and left to infuse in the cream. Careful timing is essential to guarantee the perfect balance of tastes. For both the coating and the ganache, I chose chocolates that are both gentle yet fruity, to offset the spiciness of the ginger. The match is subtle, and just as refined as the name: a Maïko is a young Japanese geisha.

Makes about 50 cookies
Preparation: 20 minutes
Cooking time: 12-15 minutes

Chocolate Cookies

Sablés au chocolat

²/₃ cup confectioners' sugar

3 tablespoons unsweetened
cocoa powder

1 stick plus 3 tablespoons unsalted
butter, softened

2 eggs

2 cups plus 1 tablespoon
all-purpose flour

¼ cup granulated sugar

1. Combine the confectioners' sugar and the cocoa powder in a bowl and mix to blend. Set aside.

2. Place the butter in a mixing bowl, add the cocoa powder mixture and beat until smooth. Add the eggs and beat vigorously. Add one third of the flour and fold just to blend with a spatula; do not overmix. Repeat for the remaining flour, adding in two more batches. Form the dough into a large ball and refrigerate for 2 hours.

3. About 30 minutes before baking, remove the dough from the refrigerator and let stand at room temperature for 10 minutes. Form the dough into little sausage shapes, about 1-inch in diameter, and roll in the granulated sugar. Return to the refrigerator for 15 minutes.

4. Meanwhile, preheat the oven to 350°. Slice the dough sausages into circles about ¼-inch thick and arrange on a nonstick baking sheet.

5. Bake for 12-15 minutes. Remove from the oven and set aside to cool before serving.

Tip: These will keep for several days in an airtight container.

Serves 5-6 people
Preparation: 10 minutes
Cooking time: 5 minutes

Chocolate Fondue

Fondue au chocolat

1. Prepare the fruit: Leave the small fruit whole; slice the apples, pears, and other large fruit. Set aside.

2. Grate the chocolate into a large heatproof bowl. Set aside. Pour the cream into a saucepan and set aside.

3. With a small knife, split the vanilla pod lengthwise down the middle. Use the tip of the knife to scrape out the seeds and stir them into the cream, along with the vanilla bean.

4. Bring the cream and vanilla to a boil over high heat. As soon as it boils, remove from the heat and pour over the grated chocolate in a thin stream. Let stand for a few seconds, then stir with a spatula using a circular motion.

5. To serve, spear the fruit with skewers, or forks, and dip quickly into the chocolate.

Tip: The chocolate can be made one day in advance and refrigerated until needed. To serve, heat over a double boiler until just warm (overheating will thicken the chocolate).

About 1 pound fruit: such as strawberries, pears, apples, bananas, mangoes, and so on
8 ounces bittersweet chocolate (4 ounces ordinary, 4 ounces orinoco)
$3/4$ cup heavy cream
$1/2$ vanilla bean

Chocolate-Orange

Chiberta

Without a doubt, this candy was a labor of attention to detail, and love. The classic combination of chocolate and orange needed a breath of fresh air, so I mixed bitter cocoa, frothy butter—for a lighter texture—and sugar rubbed against the peels of untreated oranges. This was the best way to capture the citrus flavor, without the bitterness of the pith.

I chose the name, Chiberta, after a village in the southwestern Basque region of France, because I love the carefree, sun-drenched harmony of the word.

Makes 30-35 candies

Preparation: 10 minutes

Cooking time: 3 minutes

Orangettes au chocolat

Chocolate-Coated Candied Orange Peel

$^1\!/_2$ pound candied orange peel

For the chocolate coating
$^1\!/_2$ pound bittersweet chocolate (5 ounces cuana, 3 ounces ordinary)

1. See the recipe for Tempering Chocolate (page 164) for instructions on preparing the chocolate coating.

2. Cut the orange peel into $^1\!/_2$-inch strips.

3. When the chocolate is melted (it should be warm but not boiling), spear the orange slices with a small fork and dip into the chocolate. Remove immediately, allowing the excess to drip off. Transfer to a cooling rack and refrigerate 5 minutes to harden.

Tip: Use the best orange peel you can find, which should be slightly soft. To remove the sugary coating, rinse quickly under running water, then leave to dry completely before dipping in chocolate.

Makes about 1 pound chocolates
Preparation: 20 minutes
Cooking time: 5 minutes

Chocolate-Dipped Dried Fruit

Fruits secs au chocolat

1. Prepare the chocolate coating: See the recipe for Tempering Chocolate (page 164).

2. Line a large baking sheet with aluminium foil. When the chocolate is melted and still warm (but not boiling), dip the fruit into the melted chocolate and remove using two forks. Place on the aluminium foil. Refrigerate for 5 minutes, then remove and leave to set at room temperature. The chocolate should have a hard, glossy appearance.

Tip: These candies can be kept in an airtight container.

For the chocolate coating
½ pound bittersweet chocolate (4 ounces ordinary, 4 ounces maracaïbo)

½ pound dried fruit, or candied fruit (prunes, apricots, dates, figs, orange peel, and so on)

Tarts, Pastries, and Other Baked Goods

Makes about 20 small brownies
Preparation: 20 minutes
Cooking time: 25-30 minutes

Brownies

Extra-Rich Brownies

2 ½ cups walnut pieces

½ pound bittersweet chocolate
(4 ounces maracaïbo, 4 ounces
ordinary)

7 ½ ounces unsalted butter

4 eggs

¾ cup ground almonds

Scant 1 cup granulated sugar

1 teaspoon baking soda

½ cup all-purpose flour

1. Preheat the oven to 350°.
Grease an 8x10-inch rectangular
baking pan.

2. Coarsely chop the walnuts.
Break the chocolate into pieces
and place in the top of a double
boiler to melt. Add the butter
and stir to blend. Remove from
the heat. Set aside.

3. In another bowl, combine
the eggs, ground almonds, and
sugar. Add to the melted
chocolate and stir to blend.

4. In another bowl, combine
the baking soda and flour. Sift
into the chocolate mixture. Stir
to blend. Add the walnuts and
stir again.

5. Transfer the batter to the
prepared pan and bake for
20-25 minutes. Remove from
the oven. Let stand for
5 minutes, then unmold onto
a cooling rack and cool
completely. Cut into 2-inch
squares for serving.

Tip: These are best served cold.
The brownies will keep for
several days in an airtight
container.

Makes about 10 tarts
Preparation: 45 minutes
Cooking time: about 15 minutes

Tartelettes au chocolat

Individual Chocolate Tarts

For the pastry

1 stick plus 4 tablespoons
unsalted butter

½ cup plus 1 tablespoon
confectioners' sugar

1 egg

1 egg yolk

2 cups plus 2 tablespoons
all-purpose flour

For the ganache

6 ½ ounces bittersweet chocolate
(2 ½ ounces cuana, 2 ounces
maracaïbo, 2 ounces orinoco)

2 ounces milk chocolate (merida)

½ vanilla bean

½ cup heavy cream

1. At least 5 hours before serving, prepare the pastry dough: Place the butter and sugar in a mixing bowl and rub between your fingers until the mixture resembles coarse cornmeal. Add the egg and egg yolk and work them in until combined. Add the flour and mix quickly; do not overwork the dough. Divide the dough into six pieces and roll each piece into a ball. Place the balls in a plastic bag and leave to rest in the refrigerator for 2 hours.

2. Remove the dough balls from the refrigerator and let stand at room temperature for 10 minutes. Grease 6 4-inch tart pans. Roll each ball into a circle just barely ¼-inch thick and transfer to the prepared pans. Prick the bottom all over with a fork and refrigerate for at least 3 hours (this will prevent the dough from shrinking when baked).

3. Preheat the oven to 350°. Remove the tart pans from the refrigerator. Line the bottoms with paper and fill with dried beans or pie weights. Bake for 10 minutes. Remove the paper and weights and bake until just golden. Remove from the oven and set aside to cool. (The tart shells can be made one day in advance.)

4. Prepare the ganache: Break the chocolate into pieces and place on a chopping block. Chop the pieces finely with a knife and place in a heatproof bowl. Set aside.

5. Split the vanilla bean lengthwise down the middle. Pour the cream into a saucepan, add the vanilla bean and bring to a boil. Boil for 20 seconds, then remove from the heat and pour over the chopped chocolate. Remove the vanilla bean.

6. Let stand for 30 seconds, then whisk to combine in a circular motion, starting from the middle and working out, until throughly blended. Pour into the prebaked tart shells and set aside to harden.

Tip: Do not refrigerate; this will make the pastry soggy and dry out the ganache.

Chocolate-lemon

Andalousie

Beneath a dark chocolate coating, a ganache infused with the perfume of lemon peels. A much less obvious pairing than chocolate and orange, the marriage of chocolate and lemon is also more daring. The acidity of the lemon fights with the bitterness of the chocolate, making the balance more difficult to achieve.

By combining the finest chocolates (from Venezuela, the Carribean, and Ecuador) with the best part of the lemon—the zest—we obtain an exceptional and delicate flavor, without distorting the taste of the chocolate. The aroma of these chocolates is pure and intense.

The name of this candy comes from a region in the south of Spain, where the finest lemons are grown.

Makes 15-20 choux pastries
Preparation: 55 minutes
Cooking time: 35-40 minutes

Profiteroles

Ice Cream-Filled Choux Pastries with Warm Chocolate Sauce

For the choux pastry
1 egg yolk
2 eggs
½ cup whole milk
Pinch of salt
1 teaspoon granulated sugar
3 tablespoons unsalted butter
½ cup all-purpose flour

For the chocolate ganache
¾ cup whole milk
3 ounces bittersweet chocolate
(1 ½ ounces cuana,
1 ½ ounces bloc noir)
2 tablespoons unsalted butter

Chocolate Ice Cream (see page 150)

1. Prepare the choux pastry: Preheat the oven to 400°. Grease a baking sheet. Place the egg yolk in a small dish with 1 tablespoon water and beat. Set aside.

2. Break the eggs into a mixing bowl and beat. Set aside. Place the milk, salt, sugar, and butter in a saucepan and bring to a boil. Stir with a spatula and add the flour all at once. Stir continuously. When the mixture is thoroughly blended and begins to come away from the sides of the pan, cook for a few seconds more, then remove from the heat. Add the beaten eggs gradually, in batches, stirring constantly. The mixture should be soft, but not too liquid.

3. Transfer the batter to a pastry bag fitted with a medium round tip and pipe walnut-sized mounds onto the prepared sheet, about 1½-inches apart. Brush the tops with the beaten egg yolk.

4. Bake until golden, about 20 minutes. Remove from the oven and transfer to a cooling rack. Let cool completely.

5. Prepare the chocolate ganache: Place the milk in a saucepan and bring to a boil. Meanwhile, chop the chocolate finely and place in a heatproof bowl. Pour the boiling milk over the chocolate and let stand for 30 seconds. Whisk to combine in a circular motion, starting from the middle and working out. When the chocolate has melted, add the butter in pieces. Let melt, then stir. Set aside.

6. To assemble: Just before serving, slice the choux pastries in half and fill with a scoop of chocolate ice cream. Arrange the ice cream-filled choux balls on a serving dish. Pour over the warm chocolate ganache.

Tip: You may also sprinkle the tops of the choux pastries with sliced almonds just before baking. The choux pastries will keep in the freezer. If you use frozen choux, the chocolate sauce must be poured at the very last moment.

Chocolate Pretzels

1 cup unsweetened cocoa powder
$\frac{1}{3}$ cup granulated sugar
1 stick unsalted butter, softened
2 cups plus 1 tablespoon
all-purpose flour
1 egg, beaten

For the chocolate coating
1 pound bittersweet chocolate
(ordinary)

1. Preheat the oven to 350°. Grease a baking sheet. Place the cocoa powder in a mixing bowl. Add 6 tablespoons hot water and stir to dissolve. Set aside to cool.

2. Place the butter and sugar in the bowl of an electric mixer. Beat until light and frothy. Add the cocoa mixture and beat to blend. Beat in half of the flour. Add the beaten egg and mix until blended, then beat in the remaining flour.

3. Transfer the dough to a work surface and knead until it is no longer sticky and comes away from your fingers easily. Roll into 6 thin cylinders, about 12 inches long and 1-inch in diameter. Form into pretzel shapes and place on the prepared sheet.

4. Bake for 10 minutes. Remove from the oven and set aside to cool.

5. Prepare the chocolate coating: See the recipe for Tempering Chocolate (page 164).

6. Dip the cooled pretzels into the melted chocolate and allow excess to drip off. Place on a cooling rack. Serve when the chocolate has hardened.

Makes about 8-10 éclairs
Preparation: about 45 minutes
Cooking time: 35-45 minutes

Chocolate Éclairs

Éclairs au chocolat

1. Preheat the oven to 400°. Grease a baking sheet.

2. Prepare the ganache: Grate the chocolate into a heatproof bowl. Bring the cream to a boil. Immediately pour over the chocolate. Let stand for several seconds, then stir until thoroughly melted. Set aside.

3. Prepare the choux pastry: Place the egg yolk in a small dish with 1 tablespoon water and beat. Set aside. Break the whole eggs into a mixing bowl and beat. Set aside. Place the milk, salt, sugar, and butter in a saucepan and bring to a boil. Stir with a spatula and add the flour all at once. Be sure to stir continuously. When the mixture is thoroughly blended and begins to come away from the sides of the pan, cook for a few seconds more, then remove from the heat. Add the beaten whole eggs gradually, in batches, stirring constantly. The mixture should be soft, but not too liquid.

4. Transfer the batter to a pastry bag fitted with a medium round tip. On the prepared baking sheet, pipe out lines of batter about 4 inches long and spaced about 1½ inches apart. Brush the tops with the beaten egg yolk. Bake until golden, 20-30 minutes. Remove from the oven. With a small sharp knife, make a lengthwise slit in the side of each pastry. Set aside to cool.

5. Prepare the pastry cream: Place the milk in a saucepan, add the cocoa, and bring to a boil.

For the chocolate ganache
3 ½ ounces bittersweet chocolate
(3 ounces maracaïbo, ½ ounce coro)
⅓ cup heavy cream

For the choux pastry
1 egg yolk
2 eggs
½ cup whole milk
Pinch of salt
1 teaspoon granulated sugar
3 tablespoons unsalted butter
½ cup all-purpose flour

For the pastry cream
1 cup whole milk
1 tablespoon unsweetened cocoa powder
4 egg yolks
3 tablespoons granulated sugar
3 tablespoons all-purpose flour

For the glaze
⅓ pound fondant
3 tablespoons unsweetened cocoa powder
2 tablespoons unsalted butter

6. Meanwhile, place the egg yolks in another saucepan, add the sugar, and beat until lemon-colored. Stir in the flour. Slowly pour in half of the hot milk, whisking continuously, until smooth. Add the remaining milk and place over medium heat. Cook, whisking continuously, until thick. Remove from the heat.

7. Add the ganache to the hot pastry cream and stir to blend. Set aside to cool completely; stir often to release the steam and prevent the cream from getting soggy. Fill the pastries with the cooled pastry cream, using the slit in the side.

8. Prepare the glaze: Soften the fondant in the top of a double boiler. Stir in the butter and cocoa powder. Glaze the top of each filled pastry with the chocolate mixture. Let harden before serving.

Tip: If the fondant is too thick, dilute with a few drops of water.

Variation

Chocolate Choux Pastries

Prepare the choux pastry as indicated on page 75. Transfer to a pastry bag fitted with a medium round tip. Pipe out mounds about 2-inches in diameter onto the prepared sheet and space about $1\frac{1}{2}$ inches apart. Brush the tops with the beaten egg yolk. You should have 20-25 pastries.

Bake until golden, 20-30 minutes. Remove from the oven. With the tip of a small sharp knife, make a small slit in the side of each pastry. Place on a rack to cool.

Prepare the pastry cream and glaze as indicated. Fill and glaze the choux as for the éclairs.

Makes about 15 éclairs
Preparation: about 45 minutes
Cooking time: 40-45 minutes

Caramel Éclairs

Éclairs au caramel

1. Preheat the oven to 400°. Grease a baking sheet. Prepare the choux pastry: Place the egg yolk in a small dish with 1 tablespoon water and beat. Set aside. Break the whole eggs into a mixing bowl and beat. Set aside. Place the milk, salt, sugar, and butter in a saucepan and bring to a boil. Stir with a spatula and add the flour all at once. Stir continuously. When the mixture is thoroughly blended and begins to come away from the sides of the pan, cook for a few seconds more, then remove from the heat. Add the beaten whole eggs gradually, in batches, stirring constantly. The mixture should be soft, but not too liquid.

2. Transfer the batter to a pastry bag fitted with a medium round tip. On the prepared baking sheet, pipe out lines of batter about 4 inches long and spaced about 1½ inches apart. Brush the tops with the beaten egg yolk. Bake until golden, 20-30 minutes.

3. Remove from the oven. With a small sharp knife, make a lengthwise slit in the side of each pastry. Set aside to cool. Prepare the caramel: Gradually pour the sugar into a medium-size saucepan set over low heat. Cook until the sugar begins to caramelize. As soon as it turns dark brown, remove from the heat and immediately add the cream, taking care not to splatter. Stir, then set aside to cool.

For the choux pastry
1 egg yolk
2 eggs
½ cup whole milk
Pinch of salt
1 teaspoon granulated sugar
3 tablespoons unsalted butter
½ cup all-purpose flour

For the caramel
6 tablespoons granulated sugar
6 tablespoons heavy cream

For the pastry cream
1 cup milk
2 egg yolks
2 tablespoons granulated sugar
3 tablespoons all-purpose flour

For the glaze
6 tablespoons granulated sugar
7 ounces fondant

4. Prepare the pastry cream: Place the milk in a saucepan, add 1 teaspoon of the sugar, and bring to a boil. Meanwhile, place the egg yolks in another saucepan, add the remaining sugar, and beat until lemon-colored. Stir in the flour. Slowly pour in half of the hot milk, whisking continuously, until smooth. Add the remaining milk and place over medium heat. Cook, whisking continuously, until thick. Remove from the heat. Set aside to cool completely; stir often to release steam and prevent the cream from getting soggy. When cool, stir in the caramel. Fill the pastries with the cooled caramel pastry cream, using the slit in the side.

5. Prepare the glaze: Place the sugar in a saucepan, add 6 tablespoons water, and bring to a boil. Cook for 5 minutes, until a dark caramel color. Remove from the heat, stir in the fondant and place over low heat, stirring until thoroughly blended. Set aside to cool. Glaze the top of each filled pastry with this mixture. Let harden before serving.

Tip: To test the caramel for doneness, place a few drops in a bowl of cold water. If the droplets are dark, the caramel is ready.

Variation

Caramel Choux Pastries

Prepare the choux pastry as indicated on page 77. Transfer to a pastry bag fitted with a medium round tip. Pipe out mounds about 2-inches in diameter onto the prepared sheet and space about 1½ inches apart. You should have 20-25 pastries. Brush the tops with the beaten egg yolk.

Bake until golden, 20-30 minutes. Remove from the oven. With the tip of a small sharp knife, make a small slit in the side of each pastry. Place on a rack to cool.

Prepare the pastry cream and glaze as indicated. Fill and glaze the choux as for the éclairs.

Chocolate-Rum

Beneath a slightly conical shell of milk chocolate, lies a velvety milk chocolate ganache tinged with the scent of aged, flambéed rum. This hint of aged rum lifts the flavor of the chocolate, gently tingles the palate, and makes this candy succulent. Born of fire and of passion, this chocolate deserved a heroic name, hence, I chose the opera by Gounod, one of my particular favorites.

Makes about 20 crepes
Preparation: 1 ¼ hours
Cooking time: about 15 minutes

Chocolate-Orange Crepes

For the crepes

2 cups milk

6 tablespoons unsalted butter

1 unwaxed orange

3 eggs

1 ½ tablespoons granulated sugar

Pinch of salt

1 ½ cups all-purpose flour

¼ cup orange liqueur

¼ cup rum

Unsalted butter, for cooking

For the chocolate ganache

10 ounces bittersweet chocolate
(9 ounces maracaïbo, 1 ounce cuana)

½ vanilla bean

¾ cup heavy cream

1. Prepare the crepes: Place the milk in a small saucepan and warm over low heat. Add the butter and cook until it just melts. Remove from the heat and set aside. Zest the orange. Break the eggs into a large mixing bowl. Whisk in the sugar and salt. Add half of the warmed milk, the orange zest, the orange liqueur, and the rum. Sift in the flour. Whisk to combine, then add the remaining milk and whisk to blend. Let stand for 1 hour.

2. Melt a knob of butter in an 8-inch nonstick sauté pan set over high heat. Using a ladle, transfer the batter to the hot pan and swirl to spread. Cook for 1 minute on each side. Transfer the cooked crepe to a dinner plate. Repeat until all the batter has been used, piling the crepes one on top of the other on the plate to keep them warm. You should not need additional butter for the pan after the first crepe.

3. For the chocolate ganache: With a knife, chop the chocolate finely. Transfer to a heatproof mixing bowl. Split the vanilla bean lengthwise down the middle. With a small knife, scrape out the seeds and place in a saucepan with the split bean. Add the cream and bring to a boil. Remove from the heat as soon as it boils. Let stand 20 seconds. Pour the hot cream into the chocolate in a thin stream. Wait 30 seconds, then remove the vanilla bean. Whisk to combine in a circular motion, starting from the middle and working out. Set aside.

4. To assemble: Spread the warm crepes with the chocolate ganache and serve.

Tip: These crepes are also delicious served with whipped cream.

Chocolate-Citrus

Arneguy

For this ganache, scented with the zests of grapefruit, orange, and lemon, I had to tackle their aggressive acidity in addition to the bitterness of the chocolate. After many attempts, I decided to add a few cooked cherries to the cream. The sweetness of the cherries proved the perfect foil for the acidity of the citrus fruit.

Sweet harmony: This is also the sound of the word Arneguy, a pretty village in the Basque region of France, next to the Spanish border, from which this candy gets its name.

Cakes

Serves 6-7

Preparation: 1 hour

Cooking time: about 15 minutes

Heart-Shaped Chocolate-Apricot Tart

For the pastry

1 stick plus 4 tablespoons
unsalted butter

½ cup plus 1 tablespoon
confectioners' sugar

1 egg

1 egg yolk

2 cups plus 2 tablespoons
all-purpose flour

For the apricot filling

½ cup fresh apricot purée
or apricot sauce

¼ cup confectioners' sugar

For the chocolate ganache filling

6 ½ ounces bittersweet chocolate
(3 ¼ ounces maracaïbo,
3 ¼ ounces orinoco)

2 ounces milk chocolate (merida)

½ cup heavy cream

½ vanilla bean, split

1. At least 5 hours before serving, prepare the pastry: Place the butter and sugar in a bowl and rub between your fingers until the mixture resembles coarse cornmeal. Add the egg and egg yolk and work them in until combined. Add the flour and mix quickly; do not overwork the dough. Form into a ball, place in a plastic bag, and refrigerate for at least 2 hours. (You can also prepare the pastry one day in advance).

2. Grease a heart-shaped tart pan. Remove the pastry from the refrigerator and let stand at room temperature for 10 minutes. Roll out to a ¼-inch thickness and transfer to the prepared pan. Prick the base all over with a fork and refrigerate for at least 3 hours (this prevents the pastry from shrinking during cooking).

3. Preheat the oven to 350°. Remove the pastry from the refrigerator. Line the bottom and sides with parchment paper and fill with dried beans or pie weights. Bake for 10 minutes. Remove the beans and paper, and continue cooking until just golden. Remove from the oven and let cool.

4. Prepare the apricot filling: Place the apricot purée in a saucepan. Add the sugar and bring to a boil. Cook over low heat for 5 minutes, stirring occasionally. Remove from the heat and let cool. Pour into the bottom of the pastry shell.

5. For the chocolate ganache filling: Place both the chocolates on a work surface and chop finely. Transfer to a heatproof mixing bowl and set aside. Place the cream in a saucepan, add the split vanilla bean, and bring to a boil. Boil for 20 seconds, then pour through a strainer onto the chocolate. Let stand for 30 seconds; discard the vanilla bean. Whisk to combine in a circular motion, starting from the middle and working out.

6. When the chocolate is completely melted and still lukewarm (not hot), pour over the apricot filling. Let harden before serving.

Tip: The temperature of the chocolate ganache must be correct: It should be warm enough to have a pouring consistency, but not so warm that it mixes in with the apricot filling instead of resting on top.

Chocolate Fruitcake

3 ½ ounces bittersweet chocolate (maracaïbo)

Generous ⅓ cup raisins

1 tablespoon dark rum

1 unwaxed lemon, organic if possible

½ pound unsalted butter

1 ¼ cups plus 2 tablespoons granulated sugar

8 eggs

Scant 2 cups all-purpose flour

1 ½ tablespoons unsweetened cocoa powder

1 tablespoon baking soda

7 ounces mixed candied fruit (with cherries)

2 ounces candied orange peel

Pinch of salt

1. Grease a 10-inch terrine mold and set aside in the refrigerator.

2. Finely chop the chocolate and place in the top of a double boiler set over low heat. As soon as the chocolate has melted, remove from the heat and set aside to cool.

3. Meanwhile, combine the raisins and rum and leave to soak. Remove the yellow peel from half the lemon and cut into thin slices.

4. Place the butter in a large mixing bowl and beat with a wooden spoon until creamy. Add the 1 ¼ cups sugar and mix. Pour in the melted chocolate and mix again.

5. Separate 6 of the eggs, placing the whites in a large mixing bowl. Add the yolks to the chocolate mixture, along with the 2 remaining whole eggs, and whisk to blend.

6. In another bowl, combine the flour, cocoa powder, and baking soda. Sift the dry ingredients into the chocolate mixture and stir to blend. Add the candied fruit, lemon peel, and drained raisins, and stir again. Set aside.

7. Add the salt to the egg whites and beat until they hold firm peaks. Beat in the remaining sugar until stiff and glossy. With a spatula, gently fold the beaten egg whites into the chocolate mixture. Remove the prepared mold from the refrigerator and dust with flour. Pour in the batter and let rest in a cool place for 2 hours.

8. Preheat the oven to 425°. Place the mold in the oven and bake for for 8 minutes. Lower the heat to 350° and cook for 20 minutes more.

9. Remove from the heat and unmold immediately onto a cooling rack. Let cool before serving.

Tip: If desired, soak the cake with rum immediately after removing from the oven. The heat of the cake will make the alcohol evaporate.

Biscuit moelleux au chocolat

Rich Chocolate-Almond Cake

2 ½ ounces bittersweet chocolate
(1 ounce cuana, 1 ½ ounces
ordinary)

5 tablespoons unsalted butter

¾ cup ground almonds

2 whole eggs plus 6 yolks

¾ cup plus 1 tablespoon granulated
sugar

⅓ cup cocoa powder

4 egg whites

Pinch of salt

1 teaspoon vanilla extract

1. Preheat the oven to 350°. Grease and flour an 8-inch round cake pan. Melt the chocolate in the top of a double boiler set over low heat. Add the butter and stir. When the mixture is thoroughly melted, add the ground almonds, pouring in a thin stream. Stir to blend. Remove from the heat and set aside.

2. Place the 2 whole eggs and 6 yolks in a mixing bowl with ¾ cup of the sugar and the cocoa powder. Whisk until blended, then stir into the almond-chocolate mixture. Set aside.

3. Place the 4 egg whites in the bowl of an electric mixer. Add the salt and beat until they hold stiff peaks. Add the remaining 1 tablespoon sugar and beat to combine. Gently fold the beaten whites into the chocolate mixture.

4. Transfer the batter to the prepared pan and bake. Check after 25 minutes; the cake is finished when the tip of a knife inserted in the center come out clean. If not, continue baking until done.

5. Prepare a large plate with a clean dish towel on top. Remove the cake from the oven and unmold onto the towel-covered plate. Let cool before serving.

Tip: Dust the top of the cooled cake with unsweetened cocoa powder for a more sophisticated finish.

Chocolate-Cinnamon

Cannelle

Beneath a dark chocolate exterior, a subtle, cinnamon-scented ganache. One of the most refined spices, it must always be used in stick form to obtain the best flavor. Just a hint of cinnamon, infused with cream for the correct amount of time, gently reveals the strength of the chocolate.

I love the color of this spice, and the way the word "cannelle" trips off the tongue. Its sweetly spiced, gently singing sound mirrors to perfection the blending of tastes between cinnamon and cocoa.

Serves 6-8
Preparation: 1 ½ hours
Cooking time: 25 minutes

Chocolate-Almond Cake with Lemon Cream

Andalousie

1. One day before serving, prepare the lemon cream: Place the gelatin in a dish of cold water to soften. Zest the lemon, then squeeze the juice. Strain the juice into the top of a double boiler set over low heat. Add the lemon zest and remaining ingredients, except the whipped cream. Whisk continuously until the mixture thickens. Remove from the heat. Remove the gelatin from the water and add. When the mixture is cool, transfer to a bowl and refrigerate overnight.

2. The day of serving, prepare the almond cake: Preheat the oven to 400°. Line a baking sheet with parchment paper.

3. In a large bowl, sift together the ground almonds and 1 cup confectioners' sugar. Add the cocoa powder and set aside.

4. In another mixing bowl, beat the egg whites until just firm, gradually adding the salt and the 1½ tablespoons confectioners' sugar. Transfer to the ground almond mixture and fold gently with a spatula to combine.

5. Transfer the almond batter to the prepared pan and spread evenly. Bake for 15 minutes.

6. Remove from the oven and unmold onto a cooling rack. Peel off the paper (moisten with a pastry brush dipped in water, if necessary, to help remove the paper). Let cool, then cut into 3 equal pieces. Set aside.

7. Prepare the chocolate cream: Grate the chocolate into a large heatproof mixing bowl. Place the cream in a saucepan and bring to a boil. Pour the boiling cream over the chocolate. Wait 1 minute, then stir. Refrigerate until firm.

For the lemon cream
1 sheet gelatin
2 unwaxed lemons, organic if possible
Heaping ⅓ cup granulated sugar
3 tablespoons unsalted butter
2 egg yolks
1 whole egg
½ cup plus 2 tablespoons heavy cream, whipped

For the almond cake layer
1 ½ cups ground almonds
1 cup plus 1 ½ tablespoons confectioners' sugar
⅓ cup unsweetened cocoa powder
8 egg whites
Pinch of salt

For the chocolate cream
½ pound bittersweet chocolate
(5 ½ ounces orinoco, 2 ½ ounces maracaïbo)
¼ cup heavy cream, whipped
5 tablespoons butter
¾ cup whipped cream

Chocolate Glaze (see page 166)

8. Transfer two-thirds of the chocolate mixture to the top of a double boiler set over low heat. When warm, transfer to a mixing bowl, add the butter and beat until light and fluffy. Transfer to another bowl and add the whipped cream, folding gently with a spatula. Set aside.

9. Remove the lemon cream from the refrigerator. Whisk in the whipped cream until well blended.

10. To assemble the cake, place one cake layer on a serving plate. Spread the chocolate cream evenly and top with another cake layer. Spread the second cake layer with lemon cream and top with the remaining cake layer. Refrigerate for at least 1 hour.

11. When the cake is cold, place the remaining chocolate cream in the top of a double boiler set over low heat and whisk to soften. Cover the top and sides of the cake with the chocolate cream, spreading evenly. Refrigerate for 1 hour more.

12. About 30 minutes before serving, cover the cake with Chocolate Glaze (see page 166). This cake will keep for 2-3 days in the refrigerator.

Tip: When zesting the lemon, be sure to remove only the yellow skin and not the white pith or the lemon cream may taste slightly bitter.

Lemon Pound Cake

Quatre-quarts au citron

1 unwaxed lemon, organic if possible

7 tablespoons unsalted butter

1 ³/₄ cups granulated sugar

4 eggs

¹/₃ cup heavy cream

2 cups all-purpose flour

1 tablespoon baking soda

1. Grease a 10-inch terrine mold. Dust with flour and line the bottom with parchment paper. Preheat the oven to 400°.

2. With a zesting tool or vegetable peeler, remove the yellow peel from the lemon and chop finely.

3. Combine the butter and sugar in a large mixing bowl and beat until frothy. Beat in the eggs one at a time, stirring continuously. Add the cream and beat until blended, then add the lemon zest, flour, and baking soda, and beat until incorporated.

4. Transfer to the prepared pan and bake. After 15 minutes, lower the heat to 325° and cook for 25 minutes more. The cake is finished when the tip of a knife inserted in the center come out clean. Remove from the oven. Let cool before serving.

Tip: This pound cake will keep at room temperature, covered with plastic wrap, for several days. You can serve with Chocolate Cream (page 136).

Serves 6-7

Preparation: 1 ¼ hours

Cooking time: about 25 minutes

Chocolate-Almond Cake with Rum-Raisin Ganache Icing

For the ganache

¾ cup dark raisins

¾ cup rum

10 ounces bittersweet chocolate
(5 ounces maracaïbo, 5 ounces orinoco)

1 cup heavy cream

4 tablespoons unsalted butter, softened

For the cake

1 cup plus 1 tablespoon ground almonds

¾ cup plus 1 ½ tablespoons confectioners' sugar

3 tablespoons unsweetened cocoa powder

6 egg whites

Pinch of salt

3 tablespoons granulated sugar

Chocolate Glaze (see page 166)

1. One day before making the cake, prepare the raisins: Place the raisins in a strainer and rinse under warm water. Transfer to a large bowl, add warm water to cover and leave to soak for 4 minutes. Strain, then transfer to a nonstick saucepan set over low heat. Cook, stirring constantly, until the raisins are thoroughly warmed. Remove from the heat, pour in the rum and flambée. Cover and set aside to cool.

2. Prepare the cake: Combine the ground almonds and confectioners' sugar in a mixing bowl and blend. Stir in the cocoa powder. In another bowl, combine the egg whites and salt and beat until they hold stiff peaks. Gradually add the granulated sugar and stop as soon as it is incorporated. Transfer the egg white mixture to the almond mixture and fold gently with a spatula until combined.

3. Preheat the oven to 350° and line a baking sheet with parchment paper. When the oven is hot, pour the almond batter onto the prepared baking sheet and spread into an even, ½-inch thick layer. Place in the oven and bake for 15 minutes.

4. Remove from the oven and transfer to a cooling rack; do not remove the paper. Let rest in the refrigerator for 12 hours.

5. Meanwhile, prepare the ganache: Place ½ cup of the heavy cream for the ganache in a bowl and freeze for 10 minutes. Finely chop the chocolate and place in a large heatproof bowl.

Chocolate-Raspberry

Salvador

A fresh raspberry ganache. The success of this blend depends entirely on the quality of the fruit. We use end-of-the-season raspberries, plumped with sunshine and highly perfumed. This was Maison du Chocolat's first flavored ganache, created in 1978.

To partner the lively raspberry flavor, we needed a strong, bitter dark chocolate, capable of standing up to the fruit. Hence, the name: Full of sparkling vitality, from an area that produces some of the world's finest cocoa beans.

Serves 6-7
Preparation: 1 ½ hours
Cooking time: about 20 minutes

Chocolate-Orange Layer Cake

Gounod

1. Prepare the syrup: Place the sugar in a saucepan, add the water, and bring to a boil. Cook until syrupy. Remove from the heat, stir in the orange liqueur, and set aside.

2. Prepare the cake layer: Preheat the oven to 350°. Line a baking sheet with parchment paper. Separate the eggs, placing the yolks in one mixing bowl and the whites in another mixing bowl. In another bowl, combine the flour and cocoa powder. Set aside.

3. Add all but 1 tablespoon of the sugar to the egg yolks and beat until lemon-colored. Beat in the cocoa mixture. Set aside. Add the salt to the egg whites and beat until they hold stiff peaks. Add the remaining tablespoon of sugar and beat to combine. With a spatula, gently fold the beaten egg whites into the cocoa-yolk mixture. Spread the batter evenly into the prepared sheet and bake for 7-8 minutes.

4. Remove from the oven and unmold onto another sheet of parchment paper. Peel off the paper used in cooking and set cake aside to cool.

5. Prepare the chocolate ganache: Chop the chocolate and place in a heatproof bowl. Set aside. Pour half the cream into a saucepan and bring to a boil. Pour the boiling cream onto the chopped chocolate. Let stand 1 minute, then stir until thoroughly blended. Stir in the butter. Set aside to cool. Place the remaining cream in a mixing bowl and beat until firm. Gently fold the whipped cream into the chocolate mixture. Set aside.

For the syrup
1 cup granulated sugar
¾ cup water
¼ cup orange liqueur, such as
Grand Marnier

For the cake layer
5 eggs
1 cup all-purpose flour
3 tablespoons unsweetened
cocoa powder
⅔ cup granulated sugar
Pinch of salt

For the chocolate ganache
14 ounces bittersweet chocolate
(10 ounces orinoco, 4 ounces cuana)
1 ⅔ cup heavy cream
3 tablespoons unsalted butter
⅓ pound candied orange peel,
finely diced

Chocolate Glaze (see page 166)

6. To assemble: Cut the cake layer into three equal rectangles. Moisten one side of each layer with the syrup. Refrigerate for 15 minutes.

7. Transfer one-third of the ganache to a bowl and stir in the diced orange peel. Spread evenly on top of one cake layer. Top with another cake layer and spread with half the remaining ganache mixture. Top with the remaining cake layer and refrigerate for at least 1 hour.

8. When the cake is cold, soften the remaining ganache in the top of a double boiler set over low heat. Spread the top and sides of the cake with the ganache. Refrigerate for 1 hour.

9. About 30 minutes before serving, cover the cake with Chocolate Glaze.

Tip: You may decorate the cake with candied orange peel.

Chocolate Charlotte

Charlotte au chocolat

1. One day before serving, prepare the syrup: Place the water and sugar in a saucepan and cook over low heat until syrupy. Stir in the rum and set aside to cool.

2. Prepare the chocolate cream: Place the sugar in a saucepan and add 1 tablespoon water. Cook over low heat until the mixture takes on a syrupy consistency. Set aside. Break the chocolate into pieces and melt in the top of a double boiler set over low heat.

3. Meanwhile, melt the butter in a small saucepan set over low heat. Set aside to cool. Soften the gelatin in a small bowl of cold water.

4. Place the egg whites in a large mixing bowl and beat until they hold stiff peaks. Gradually pour in the sugar-water mixture, beating constantly, until combined. Remove the gelatin from the water, shake off the excess water, and beat into the egg whites.

5. Combine the melted chocolate and the butter. Transfer to the egg whites, folding gently with a spatula until smooth.

6. To assemble: Moisten 4 ladyfingers with the rum syrup and arrange in the bottom of a 7-inch charlotte mold. Top with a thin 1-inch layer of chocolate cream. Continue layering moistened ladyfingers and chocolate cream until the mold is full, ending with a layer of ladyfingers. Refrigerate the Charlotte and the remaining chocolate cream for 12 hours. Reserve the remaining syrup.

7. Just before serving, unmold the Charlotte onto a serving plate. Surround with the remaining chocolate cream. Moisten the remaining ladyfingers with syrup and arrange around the Charlotte.

8. Prepare the whipped cream: Place the chilled cream in a large mixing bowl. Add the sugar and beat until it forms soft peaks. Serve the Charlotte with the whipped cream on the side.

Tip: This Charlotte may also be served with Chocolate Custard Sauce (see page 141) or with mixed berries.

For the rum syrup
1 cup water
³/₄ cup granulated sugar
6 tablespoons rum

For the chocolate cream
1 ¹/₄ cups granulated sugar
¹/₂ pound bittersweet chocolate
(6 ounces ordinary, 2 ounces orinoco)
7 tablespoons unsalted butter
5 egg whites
3 gelatin sheets
¹/₂ pound ladyfingers

For the whipped cream
1 cup heavy cream, chilled
1 tablespoon granulated sugar

Serves 6-7
Preparation: 1 ½ hours
Cooking time: about 20 minutes

Moccambo

Chocolate-Raspberry Cake

For the cake layer

1 cup plus 1 tablespoon ground almonds

¾ cup plus 1 ½ tablespoons
confectioners' sugar

3 tablespoons unsweetened
cocoa powder

6 egg whites

Pinch of salt

3 tablespoons granulated sugar

For the chocolate ganache

10 ounces bittersweet chocolate
(7 ounces maracaïbo, 3 ounces orinoco)

½ cup heavy cream

4 tablespoons unsalted butter

3 ½ ounces fresh raspberries

1 tablespoon granulated sugar

Chocolate Glaze (see page 166)

1. One day before serving, prepare the cake layer: Line a baking sheet with parchment paper. Preheat the oven to 350°. In a large mixing bowl, combine the ground almonds, confectioners' sugar, and cocoa powder. Stir to blend.

2. In another mixing bowl, combine the egg whites and salt and beat until they hold stiff peaks. Add the sugar and beat for a few seconds more. Carefully transfer the beaten egg whites to the ground almond mixture, folding gently but thoroughly with a spatula.

3. Spread the batter evenly in the prepared baking sheet. Bake for 15 minutes. Remove from the oven and let cool on a cooling rack. Refrigerate for 12 hours; do not remove the paper.

4. Meanwhile, prepare the chocolate ganache: Finely chop the chocolate and place in a heatproof mixing bowl. Place the cream in a saucepan, bring to a boil, then pour the boiling cream onto the chopped chocolate. Let stand for 1 minute, then stir until thoroughly blended. Refrigerate for 2 hours.

5. Transfer two-thirds of the ganache to the top of a double boiler set over low heat. When warm, stir in the butter, and let stand at room temperature for 12 hours.

6. The day of serving, assemble the cake: Remove the cake from the refrigerator and peel off the paper. Cut lengthwise into 3 even pieces. Combine the raspberries and sugar and crush to obtain a coarse purée.

7. With a pastry brush, moisten the 3 cake layers with the raspberry purée. With an electric mixer, beat the chocolate-butter ganache for 2-3 minutes. Spread two of the three cake layers with an even layer of the whipped chocolate-butter mixture. Spread the raspberry purée on top of the chocolate. Place one of the chocolate-raspberry layers on top of the other (cake, chocolate, raspberry topped with cake, chocolate, raspberry) and top with the remaining plain cake layer. Refrigerate for 1 hour.

8. When the cake is cold, soften the remaining ganache in the top of a double boiler set over low heat. Spread over the top and sides of the cake, then return to the refrigerator for 1 hour more.

9. About 30 minutes before serving, cover the cake with Chocolate Glaze.

Tip: You may also serve this cake with a raspberry sauce and decorate the top with fresh raspberries.

Chocolate-Fennel

Garrigue

Beneath a dark chocolate coating, a fennel-scented ganache. We begin by lightly crushing the fennel stems and seeds, followed by a precise infusing time. It must be just right to keep the balance: Too much, and the fennel will overpower the chocolate.

This daring blend requires precision to balance the explosive aromas, reminiscent of the sun-baked landscape of Provence.

Serves 6
Preparation: 20 minutes
Cooking time: about 20 minutes

Pleyel Simple Chocolate-Almond Cake

½ vanilla bean

7 ounces bittersweet chocolate

(3 ½ ounces ordinary, 3 ½ ounces

cuana)

5 eggs

1 stick plus 4 tablespoons

unsalted butter

1 ⅔ cup confectioners' sugar

Pinch of salt

1 ½ tablespoons granulated sugar

¾ cup all-purpose flour

¾ cup ground almonds

1. Split the vanilla bean lengthwise down the middle. With a small knife, scrape out the seeds and place in the top of a double boiler, along with the split bean. Break the chocolate into small pieces and add to the vanilla. Melt over low heat.

2. Separate the eggs, putting the whites into a large mixing bowl and the yolks in a smaller bowl.

3. When the chocolate is melted, add the butter in pieces and stir to blend. Stir in the confectioners' sugar and egg yolks. Stir in the ground almonds and remove from the heat. Add the flour and mix well. Set aside.

4. Preheat the oven to 400°. Grease and flour a 10-inch terrine mold. Add the salt to the egg whites, then beat until they hold stiff peaks. Gradually beat in the granulated sugar. Fold the egg whites into the chocolate mixture until thoroughly combined.

5. Pour the batter into the prepared pan and bake for about 20 minutes. The cake is finished when the tip of a knife inserted in the center come out clean.

6. Remove from the oven and unmold onto a serving plate. Let cool slightly before serving.

Tip: This cake will keep for 3 days, covered with plastic wrap.

Serves 6-7

Preparation: 1 ¼ hours

Cooking time: about 20 minutes

Délice

Chocolate-Almond Cake

For the chocolate-almond cake layer

1 cup plus 1 tablespoon ground almonds

¾ cup plus 1 ½ tablespoon confectioners' sugar

3 tablespoons unsweetened cocoa powder

6 egg whites

Pinch of salt

2 heaping tablespoons granulated sugar

For the chocolate ganache

10 ounces bittersweet chocolate (5 ounces ordinary, 5 ounces cuana)

⅓ cup heavy cream

3 rounded tablespoons unsalted butter

Chocolate Glaze (see page 166)

1. One day before serving, prepare the almond cake layer: Preheat the oven to 350°. Line a baking sheet with parchment paper. In a large mixing bowl, combine the ground almonds and confectioners' sugar. Add the cocoa powder and stir to blend. In another large bowl, combine the egg whites and salt and beat until they hold stiff peaks. Quickly add the sugar and beat again until just blended. Transfer the almond mixture to the beaten egg whites and fold gently until thoroughly blended.

2. Transfer to the prepared baking sheet and spread evenly. Bake for 15 minutes. Remove from the oven and unmold onto a cooling rack. Refrigerate for 12 hours; do not remove the parchment paper.

3. Meanwhile, prepare the chocolate ganache: Finely chop the chocolate and place in a large heatproof bowl. Place the cream in a saucepan; bring to a boil. Pour the boiling cream over the chopped chocolate. Let stand 1 minute, then stir. Refrigerate for 2 hours.

4. Transfer two-thirds of the ganache to the top of a double boiler set over low heat. When warm, gradually add the butter and mix. Remove from the heat and let stand at room temperature for 12 hours.

5. The day of serving, remove the paper from the cake and cut into 3 equal rectangles.

6. With an electric mixer, beat the ganache for 3 minutes. Spread one cake layer with one-third of the ganache. Top with a cake layer and repeat. Place the remaining cake layer on top and refrigerate for 1 hour.

7. When the cake is cold, soften the remaining ganache in the top of a double boiler set over low heat. Cover the top and sides of the cake with the softened ganache, then refrigerate for 1 hour more.

8. About 30 minutes before serving, cover the cake with Chocolate Glaze.

Tip: You may also serve this cake with Chocolate Custard Sauce (see page 141).

Serves 8-10
Preparation: 1 ½ hours
Cooking time: about 15 minutes

Bûche Isabella

Chocolate-Pear Layer Cake

For the cake layer
4 eggs
¾ cup all-purpose flour
2 ½ tablespoons unsweetened
cocoa powder
½ cup plus 1 tablespoon granulated
sugar
Pinch of salt

For the syrup
¾ cup granulated sugar
⅔ cup water
2 tablespoons pear eau de vie

For the dark chocolate ganache
7 ounces bittersweet chocolate
(5 ounces orinoco, 2 ounces maracaïbo)
¾ cup heavy cream
½ vanilla bean

For the milk chocolate ganache
7 ½ ounces bittersweet chocolate
(6 ounces merida, 1 ½ ounces
maracaïbo)
¾ cup whipping cream
1 gelatin sheet

3 canned pears, syrup reserved

Chocolate Glaze (see page 166)

1. Prepare the cake layer: Preheat the oven to 350°. Line a baking sheet with parchment paper. Separate the eggs, placing the yolks in one bowl and the whites in a large mixing bowl. In another bowl, combine the flour and cocoa powder. Add ½ cup of the sugar to the egg yolks and beat until lemon-colored. Stir in the cocoa-flour mixture. Add the salt to the egg whites and beat until they hold stiff peaks. Add the remaining 1 tablespoon sugar and beat to combine. With a spatula, gently fold the whites into the cocoa-yolk mixture until well blended. Spread the batter evenly in the prepared pan and bake for 7-8 minutes.

2. Meanwhile, prepare the syrup: Place the sugar in a saucepan and add the water. Bring to a boil and cook until syrupy. Remove from the heat and add the pear eau de vie. Set aside.

3. Remove the cake from the oven and unmold onto another sheet of parchment paper. Wait for several seconds, then peel off the paper used in cooking. Set aside to cool.

4. Prepare the dark chocolate ganache: Finely chop the chocolate and place in a heatproof bowl. Split the vanilla bean lengthwise down the middle. With the tip of a small knife, scrape out the beans into a saucepan. Add ⅔ cup of the cream to the saucepan and bring to a boil. Pour the boiling cream on the chocolate. Let stand 1 minute, then stir until well blended. Set aside to cool. Place the remaining cream in a mixing bowl and beat until firm. Gently fold the whipped cream into the cooled chocolate mixture. Set aside.

5. To assemble: Cut the cake into 3 equal rectangles. Moisten one side of each cake piece with syrup. Place one cake layer on a serving plate and spread with two-thirds of the dark chocolate ganache. Set aside to harden.

6. Prepare the milk chocolate ganache: Place the gelatin sheet in cold water to soften. Chop the chocolate and place in a heatproof bowl. Place half of the cream in a saucepan and bring to a boil. Drain the softened gelatin sheets and add to the cream. Set aside to melt the

122

gelatin, then pour over the chopped chocolate. Let stand 1 minute, then stir to blend. Set aside to cool. Pour the remaining cream in a mixing bowl and beat until firm. Gently fold the whipped cream into the cooled chocolate mixture. Set aside.

7. Drain the pears and slice thinly lengthwise. When the first layer of dark chocolate ganache has hardened, arrange half the pear slices on top. Cover with another cake layer. Spread the top with all of the milk chocolate ganache and let stand to harden for a few minutes. Arrange the remaining pear slices on top and cover with the last cake layer. Refrigerate for 1 hour.

8. Soften the remaining dark chocolate ganache in the top of a double boiler set over low heat; do not melt. Spread over the top and sides of the cake and refrigerate for 1 hour.

9. Meanwhile, prepare the Chocolate Glaze and pour over the cake while still lukewarm.

Chocolate-Pistachio

Jolika

Coated with bittersweet chocolate, decorated with a sprinkling of pistachio. The marzipan interior is balanced with finely ground pistachios and a hint of kirsch, for refinement. The resulting blend is highly perfumed and not too sweet. This candy is named after a pistachio cake, which I learned to make as a young apprentice in Switzerland.

Serves 6
Preparation: 1 ½ hours
Cooking time: 30 minutes

Gâteau moelleux aux pommes

Rich Chocolate-Honey Cake with Apples

For the syrup
1 cup water
¾ cup granulated sugar
1 tablespoon dark rum

For the cake layer
1 cup all-purpose flour
3 tablespoons unsweetened
cocoa powder
4 eggs
½ cup granulated sugar

For the chocolate ganache
½ pound bittersweet chocolate
(6 ounces orinoco, 2 ounces ordinary)
1 cup heavy cream
3 tablespoons unsalted butter
3 tablespoons rum
1 cup heavy cream, whipped
3 tablespoons honey

For the apples
4 apples, such as Gala
¾ cup granulated sugar

Chocolate Glaze (see page 166)

1. Prepare the syrup: Place the water in a saucepan, add the sugar and bring to a boil. Cook until syrupy, about 5 minutes. Remove from the heat and stir in the rum. Set aside.

2. Prepare the cake: Preheat the oven to 350°. Grease an 8-inch springform pan.

3. In the bowl of an electric mixer, combine the eggs and sugar and beat until the mixture is thick and falls like a ribbon from the beaters. Add the flour and cocoa powder, and fold gently to combine.

4. Transfer to the prepared pan and bake for 15 minutes. When the cake is cooked, remove from the oven, unmold, and let stand at room temperature for a few minutes. Cover with a damp dish towel and set aside to cool completely.

5. To prepare the chocolate ganache: Finely chop the chocolate and place in a bowl that is heatproof. In a saucepan, combine the cream and honey and bring to a boil. Slowly pour the hot cream mixture over the chopped chocolate. Wait 20 seconds, then stir until well blended. Stir in the butter and the rum. Add the whipped cream and mix well. Set aside.

6. To assemble the cake: Slice the cooled cake horizontally into 3 even pieces. With a pastry brush, moisten each of the cake pieces with the syrup. Place one layer on a serving dish and spread with one-third of the ganache. Top with another cake layer and spread over half the remaining ganache. Top with the remaining cake layer. Refrigerate for 1 hour.

7. When the cake is cold, soften the remaining ganache in the top of a double boiler set over low heat. Cover the top and sides of the cake with the softened ganache. Refrigerate for 1 hour more.

8. About 30 minutes before serving, cover the cake with the Chocolate Glaze.

9. Peel the apples and slice into quarters. Remove the core and slice each quarter in half. Place the sugar in a large nonstick saute pan. Add the apple slices and cook over high heat, until the apples are caramelized. Arrange the hot apples around the cake and serve.

Tip: Serve this cake with a dessert wine from Banyuls.

Decadent Chocolate Dessert

Marquise au chocolat

1. One day before serving, grease a round 8-inch cake pan. Break the chocolate into pieces, place in the top of a double boiler, and melt over a low heat.
2. Meanwhile, separate the eggs, placing the whites in a large mixing bowl. Leave the yolks in their half-shells. Set aside.
3. Place the butter and ½ cup of the sugar in a mixing bowl and beat until light and frothy. Add the yolks, one at a time. Stir in the chocolate. Set aside.

4. Beat the egg whites with the remaining ¼ cup sugar until they hold stiff peaks. Gently fold the beaten whites into the chocolate mixture. The mixture should be well blended, but overmixing will deflate the beaten egg whites. Transfer to the prepared pan. Place a weight on top. Refrigerate for 12 hours.
5. Just before serving, whip the cream with the confectioners' sugar until it holds soft peaks.
6. Unmold the dessert, cut into slices, and serve with the whipped cream.

12 ounces bittersweet chocolate
(8 ounces orinoco, 4 ounces ordinary)
4 eggs
1 stick plus 4 tablespoons
unsalted butter
¾ cup granulated sugar
¾ cup heavy cream
¼ cup confectioners' sugar

Chocolate-Almond

Traviata

Beneath a dark chocolate coating, an almond praline covered with lightly caramelized chopped almonds and hazelnuts. For the praline, the balance of flavors relies on just the right amount of almond to enhance its true aroma. We blanch the almonds and hazelnuts to remove all traces of bitterness.

The dramatic tones of this candy instantly reminded me of the theatrical character from Giuseppe Verdi's *The Lady of the Camelias*.

Gâteau aux marrons

Chocolate Chestnut Cake

For the syrup

2 cups water

1 ½ cups sugar

3 tablespoons rum

For the chocolate genoise

1 cup all-purpose flour

3 tablespoons unsweetened

cocoa powder

5 eggs

⅔ cup granulated sugar

For the filling

2 cups rum

1 ⅛ pounds chestnut paste

(unsweetened)

1 ⅛ pounds chestnut cream

(crème de marrons)

1 stick plus 2 tablespoons

unsalted butter, softened

¾ cup heavy cream

1. Prepare the syrup: Combine the water and sugar in a saucepan set over low heat and cook just until the sugar melts. Stir in the rum and remove from the heat.

2. Prepare the genoise: Preheat the oven to 425°. Line an 8 x 10-inch rectangular cake pan with parchment paper.

3. Combine the flour and cocoa powder in a mixing bowl. Set aside. Place the eggs and sugar in another bowl and whisk until the mixture is thick and falls like a ribbon from the beaters. Add the cocoa powder mixture and gently fold in with a spatula.

4. Pour the batter into the prepared pan, spread evenly, and bake for 5 minutes. Reduce the heat to 350° and bake for 3-4 minutes more. Remove from the oven, let cool, then unmold onto a sheet of parchment paper. Peel off the paper used in baking (moisten if necessary to help remove it). Cover with a damp dish towel to keep moist and leave to cool.

5. Prepare the filling: Warm the rum in a small saucepan. In a mixing bowl, combine the chestnut paste, chestnut cream, softened butter, and warm rum and beat until thoroughly combined. Transfer to a large mixing bowl and set aside.

6. Whip the cream until it just holds peaks. Add to the chestnut mixture and fold in gently.

7. To assemble the cake: Cut the genoise into three equal rectangles. Place one rectangle on a serving plate and moisten with one-third of the rum syrup. Spread over one-third of the chestnut mixture, sprinkle over the chestnut pieces, and cover with a second genoise rectangle. Moisten the top cake layer with half the remaining syrup, then spread with half the remaining chestnut mixture. Top with the last genoise rectangle.

8. Spread the top layer with the remaining chestnut mixture and decorate as desired. Refrigerate for at least 1 hour before serving. Slice thinly to serve.

Tip: Let the cake stand at room temperature for at least 30 minutes before serving. If desired, you can cover the top with Chocolate Glaze (see page 166).

Epiphany Cake

Galette des rois

For the ganache
1 pound bittersweet chocolate
(8 ounces maracaïbo,
8 ounces orinoco)
2 cups heavy cream
1 vanilla bean
1 small candy, preferably chocolate

For the pastry
1/2 pound all-butter puff pastry
1 egg yolk, beaten

1. One day before serving, prepare the chocolate filling: Finely chop the chocolate and place in a heatproof bowl. Pour the heavy cream into a saucepan. With a small knife, split the vanilla bean lengthwise down the middle and scrape out the little black seeds into the pan of cream. Bring to a boil. Pour the boiling cream over the chopped chocolate and discard the vanilla bean. Let stand for a few seconds, then stir until thoroughly combined. Set aside in a cool place for 12 hours (do not refrigerate).

2. The day of serving, prepare the pastry: Roll out the pastry into a circle about 10-12 inches in diameter. Transfer to a baking sheet lined with parchment paper and refrigerate for 2 hours.

3. Preheat the oven to 425°. Remove the pastry from the refrigerator. Brush the top with the egg yolk. With the tip of a small knife, cut a criss-cross pattern on top. Pierce 5-6 times to allow steam to escape.

4. Bake until golden, about 20 minutes. Remove from the oven and transfer to a cooling rack. Let cool.

5. To assemble: Place the ganache in the top of a double boiler to soften, whisking until soft and frothy.

6. Spread the ganache over one circle and place the candy on top. Let stand 5 minutes to harden. Cover with the top pastry circle and let stand 1-2 hours.

7. Just before serving, preheat the oven to 400°. As soon as the oven reaches temperature, turn it off. Place the cake in the hot oven for 5-7 minutes, just to warm (the ganache should not melt). Serve immediately.

Note: This cake is traditionally served on the 6th of January to celebrate Epiphany. A fève, or small porcelain figurine, is baked into the cake. Whoever gets the portion with the fève wears the golden paper crown that adorns the cake. The traditional filling is almond; this recipe is a chocolate variation.

Creams,
Mousses,
Custards,
and
Soufflés

Crème chocolat

Chocolate Cream

10 ounces bittersweet chocolate
(5 ounces orinoco,
5 ounces maracaïbo)

3 egg yolks

$\frac{1}{2}$ cup granulated sugar

2 cups whole milk

$\frac{1}{2}$ vanilla bean

$\frac{1}{2}$ cup unsweetened cocoa powder

$\frac{1}{2}$ cup heavy cream, whipped

1. Break the chocolate into chunks. Place on a chopping board and chop finely with a large knife.

2. In a large mixing bowl, combine the egg yolks and sugar and beat with an electric mixer until thick and lemon-colored. Add 1 cup of the milk and stir.

3. Pour the remaining 1 cup milk into a saucepan and bring to a boil. Meanwhile, split the vanilla bean lengthwise down the middle and use a small knife to scrape out the seeds. Add the vanilla seeds, bean, and the cocoa to the saucepan. Lower the heat and stir continuously with a wooden spoon until the mixture is thick enough to coat the back of the spoon.

4. Place a fine-mesh strainer over a large heatproof bowl and pour in the hot milk mixture. Discard the vanilla bean and seeds. Stir in the chopped chocolate until completely melted, then set aside to cool, stirring occasionally. Refrigerate for 1 hour.

5. Whip the cream. Add one-third of the chocolate mixture to the whipped cream. Fold gently to combine, then transfer the cream-chocolate mixture to the remaining chocolate and fold gently until well blended. Serve chilled.

Tip: This Chocolate Cream can also be served with the Lemon Pound Cake or Chocolate Chip Tile Cookies.

Chocolate-Vanilla

Beneath a coating of dark chocolate, a semisweet ganache. The full-flavored aroma is the result of blending cocoa beans from Ecuador, Venezuela, and Indonesia. To balance these powerful tastes, I added vanilla, which brings a note of femininity and a lingering taste on the palate. The result remains subtle, velvety, and full-flavored, but not overpowering.

This candy is part of a series of chocolates that take their names from the origins of their ingredients. This was the first of our South American candies, hence the name of an Ecuadorian port town.

Souffle au chocolat

Chocolate Soufflé

6 eggs

7 ounces bittersweet chocolate

(3 ½ ounces ordinary,

3 ½ ounces orinoco)

1 vanilla bean

1 ¾ cup plus 1 tablespoon granulated

sugar

4 tablespoons potato starch

Unsweetened cocoa powder,

for dusting

1. Butter a 10-inch soufflé dish and set aside.

2. Separate the eggs, placing the whites in a large mixing bowl and leaving each yolk in its half-shell.

3. Chop or break the chocolate into small pieces. Split the vanilla bean lengthwise down the middle and scrape out the seeds with a small knife. Place the vanilla seeds, bean, and chocolate pieces in the top of a double boiler set over low heat and leave to melt, stirring occasionally.

4. Preheat the oven to 400°. When the chocolate is melted, add half the egg yolks and stir to blend. Add the remaining yolks and stir to blend. Stir in 1 cup of the sugar and the potato starch. Remove from the heat.

5. Beat the egg whites, gradually adding the remaining sugar, until they hold stiff peaks. Gently fold the egg whites into the chocolate mixture. The mixture should be well blended, but overmixing will deflate the beaten egg whites.

6. Coat the inside of the buttered soufflé dish with a thin layer of flour. Pour in the chocolate-egg mixture, filling to just below the rim.

7. Bake for 25 minutes. Remove from the oven.

8. To serve, place the cocoa powder in a small strainer and sift over the top of the soufflé. Serve immediately.

Tip: To test the soufflé for doneness, pierce the center with a needle; it should come out completely clean.

1. Prepare the chocolate custard sauce: Finely chop the chocolate and place in a large heatproof bowl. Set aside. Split the vanilla bean lengthwise. Place the milk in a saucepan, add the vanilla bean, and bring to a boil. Remove from the heat and set aside.

2. Place the egg yolks in a large mixing bowl. Add the sugar and whisk until lemon-colored. Slowly pour in the hot milk, whisking constantly. Pour the milk-egg mixture back into the saucepan and cook over low heat, stirring constantly, until it is thick enough to coat the back of the spoon, about 3-4 minutes. Pour over the chopped chocolate and stir to blend.

3. Transfer to a large serving bowl. Remove the vanilla bean and let cool. Refrigerate until needed.

4. Prepare the snow eggs: Beat the egg whites until they hold firm peaks. Meanwhile, fill a large saucepan with water and bring to a boil, then lower the heat and simmer gently. Place a clean dish towel on the work surface. Using a large soup spoon, scoop out a heaping spoonful of beaten egg white and place carefully in the simmering water. Let cook for 2 minutes, then remove with a slotted spoon and place on the dish towel to drain. Repeat with the remaining egg whites.

5. Prepare the caramel: Place a saucepan over low heat and add 1 tablespoon water. Slowly pour in the sugar and let melt, stirring occasionally, until the sugar turns a deep brown color. Remove from the heat and set aside.

6. To serve, arrange the snow eggs on top of the chocolate custard and drizzle over the caramel. Sprinkle over the cocoa powder. Serve immediately.

Chocolate Snow Eggs

Œufs à la neige au chocolat

For the chocolate custard sauce
1/3 pound bittersweet chocolate
(3 1/2 ounces maracaïbo,
1 1/2 ounces ordinary)
1/2 vanilla bean
2 cups whole milk
4 egg yolks
1/2 cup granulated sugar

For the snow eggs and caramel
4 egg whites
1 1/4 cups granulated sugar
1 tablespoon unsweetened
cocoa powder, to decorate

Mousse au chocolat nature

Bittersweet Chocolate Mousse

14 ounces bittersweet chocolate
(5 ounces orinoco, 4 ½ ounces
maracaïbo, 4 ½ ounces cuana)

5 tablespoons unsalted butter,
softened

4 egg yolks

1 vanilla bean

6 tablespoons heavy cream

1 ½ tablespoons unsweetened
cocoa powder

10 egg whites

1 ½ tablespoons granulated sugar

1. Finely chop the chocolate and place in the top of a double boiler set over low heat. When the chocolate is melted, add the butter and stir to blend. Whisk in the egg yolks until they are thoroughly blended.

2. Split the vanilla bean lengthwise down the middle. In a saucepan, combine the cream, cocoa, and vanilla bean over low heat. Cook until warm.

3. Remove the chocolate-egg mixture from the heat. Pour the cream mixture through a strainer held over the chocolate and stir to blend. Discard the vanilla bean and set aside.

4. In a large bowl, beat the egg whites, gradually adding the sugar, until they hold stiff peaks. Fold the egg whites into the chocolate mixture with a wooden spoon. Overmixing will deflate the egg whites, but make sure the mixture is well combined.

5. Transfer to a serving dish and refrigerate for at least 1 hour. Remove from the refrigerator 10-15 minutes before serving; the mousse should not be too hard or too cold.

Tip: Serve with Chocolate Cookies (see page 54).

Variation

Milk Chocolate Mousse

Replace the chocolate quantity with 4 ounces bittersweet chocolate and 10 ounces milk chocolate (merida). The other ingredients and preparation remain the same.

Mousse au chocolat à la framboise

Chocolate-Raspberry Mousse

4 eggs

14 ounces bittersweet chocolate
(7 ounces ordinary, 7 ounces
maracaïbo)

½ cup raspberry preserves (or jelly)

5 tablespoons unsalted butter

6 egg whites

Pinch of salt

1 ½ tablespoons granulated sugar

1 ½ tablespoons unsweetened
cocoa powder

1. Separate the 4 whole eggs, placing the yolks in a small dish and the whites in a large mixing bowl. Set aside.

2. Finely chop the chocolate and place in the top of a double boiler set over low heat and leave to melt.

3. When the chocolate has melted, gently stir in the raspberry preserves. Stir in the butter, cut in pieces, and mix gently. Add the egg yolks, one at a time, whisking after each addition. Whisk until the mixture is thoroughly blended, then remove from the heat.

4. Add the salt to the egg whites and beat, gradually adding the sugar, until they hold stiff peaks. Gently fold in the cocoa with a rubber spatula.

5. Add half the beaten egg whites to the melted chocolate mixture and mix well. Transfer the egg-chocolate mixture to the bowl with the remaining beaten egg whites and fold, lifting the mixture gently to blend. The mixture should be well blended, but overmixing will deflate the beaten egg whites.

6. Transfer to a serving dish and refrigerate until firm but not hard. Let stand at room temperature for a few minutes before serving; the mousse should not be too cold.

Tip: For an even richer dessert, replace the preserves with strained, fresh raspberry pulp and decorate with whole fresh raspberries.

Chocolate-Hazelnut

Figaro

Beneath a layer of dark chocolate, this candy brings together hazelnuts, almonds, and caramel. The nuts are thoroughly blanched to remove all traces of bitterness, then ground and thrown into the caramel. The balance of flavors relies partly on the caramel;overcooked and it becomes bitter, undercooked, and it is too sweet. I also increased the quantity of almonds in relation to hazelnuts, which are stronger, resulting in a chocolate that is supremely delicate.

This candy is not very sweet, but it is light and lilting, like its namesake by Mozart and Rossini.

Frozen Desserts and Beverages

Makes about 2 quarts
Preparation: 25 minutes
Cooking time: 10 minutes

Chocolate Ice Cream

½ pound bittersweet chocolate
(4 ounces ordinary, 4 ounces cuana)
1 quart whole milk
⅓ cup unsweetened cocoa powder
¾ cup granulated sugar
7 egg yolks
1 whole egg
¾ cup heavy cream

1. Finely chop the chocolate and set aside.

2. In a saucepan, combine the milk, cocoa powder, and ¼ cup of the sugar. Stir to blend, then warm over low heat.

3. Meanwhile, combine the egg yolks, whole egg, and the remaining ½ cup sugar in a mixing bowl. Beat until frothy and lemon-colored.

4. Pour a little bit of hot chocolate milk onto the egg mixture and stir well. Transfer the milk-egg mixture back to the saucepan of milk and cook over low heat, stirring constantly with a wooden spoon, until thick enough to coat the back of the spoon; do not boil.

5. Remove from the heat and stir in the chopped chocolate until completely melted. Stir in the heavy cream.

6. Set aside to cool, stirring occasionally. Freeze in an ice cream machine according to manufacturer's instructions.

Tip: To serve at just the right consistency, transfer the ice cream from the freezer to the refrigerator ½ hour before serving.

Serves 6

Preparation: 25 minutes

Cooking time: 10 minutes

Chestnut Ice Cream

Glace aux marrons

1 vanilla bean

1 quart whole milk

1 cup heavy cream

$^3/_4$ cup granulated sugar

8 egg yolks

$^1/_2$ pound chestnut purée

$^1/_2$ pound chestnut paste

1. Prepare a custard sauce base: Split the vanilla bean lengthwise down the middle. In a saucepan, combine the milk, heavy cream, $^1/_4$ cup of the sugar, and the vanilla bean. Bring to a boil, then remove from the heat and set aside to infuse.

2. In a mixing bowl, combine the egg yolks and the remaining $^1/_2$ cup sugar and beat until frothy and lemon-colored. Add the warm milk, pouring in a thin stream, stirring constantly with a wooden spoon.

3. Return the mixture to the saucepan and place over medium heat. Cook, stirring constantly with a wooden spoon, until the mixture is thick enough to coat the back of the spoon. Remove from the heat.

4. Place the chestnut purée and paste in a heatproof mixing bowl. Pour in the hot milk through a strainer and stir to blend. Set aside to cool, stirring occasionally.

5. Freeze in an ice cream machine according to the manufacturer's instructions.

Tip: To enhance the chestnut flavor, add 1 tablespoon of flambéed rum to the custard sauce base before infusing. You may also add chopped candied chestnuts to the ice cream before it is completely frozen.

Chocolate-tea

Yoko

A tea-scented ganache. This required a strong flavor that could stand up to the chocolate, so we chose two: Earl Grey, and a smoky black tea from China, Lapsang Souchong.

The name of this candy comes from one of the great tea empires: Japan.

Makes about 2 quarts
Preparation: 20 minutes
Cooking time: 10 minutes

Sorbet chocolat

Chocolate Sorbet

10 ounces bittersweet chocolate
(3 $^1/_3$ ounces cuana, 3 $^1/_3$ ounces
orinoco, 3 $^1/_3$ ounces maracaïbo)
2 tablespoons vanilla extract
(or $^1/_2$ vanilla bean)
1 quart water
1 $^1/_4$ cups granulated sugar
$^1/_2$ cup unsweetened cocoa powder

1. Finely chop the chocolate. If using the vanilla bean, split lengthwise down the middle. With the tip of a small knife, scrape out the seeds into a saucepan. Add the water, sugar, cocoa powder, and vanilla bean.
2. Prepare a large, shallow baking dish half full of water. Bring the cocoa mixture to a boil, and boil for 5 minutes. Add the chopped chocolate, whisking to combine and thoroughly melt the chocolate. As soon as the mixture returns to a boil, remove from the heat and place the saucepan in the dish of water to cool down quickly. Remove the vanilla bean.

3. Freeze in an ice cream machine according to the manufacturer's instructions.

Tip: The sorbet is best served slightly softened; remove from the freezer 15-20 minutes before serving for best results.

1. Finely chop the chocolate. In a saucepan, combine the milk, water, cocoa powder, and vanilla bean, if using, and bring to a boil. As soon as the mixture boils, add the chopped chocolate and cook over low heat, stirring occasionally.

2. Pour the chocolate milk through a fine-mesh strainer set over another saucepan. Set aside to cool, stirring occasionally.

3. Just before serving, reheat the chocolate so that it is warm, but not boiling.

Tip: Prepare the drink several hours in advance to intensify the flavor and texture of the chocolate.

Variations

Hot Chocolate with Coffee

Prepare as for the hot chocolate, but add 6 tablespoons strong black coffee, then leave to cool.

Hot Chocolate with Cinnamon

Add a few cinnamon sticks to the milk, and add the water and cocoa powder. Bring to a boil and cook for 15 minutes. Pour through a strainer before serving.

Hot Chocolate with Rum

Prepare as for hot chocolate, but add 3 tablespoons rum just before serving.

Hot Chocolate

Chocolat chaud nature

7 ounces bittersweet chocolate
(3 ½ ounces ordinary,
3 ½ ounces maracaïbo)
2 cups whole milk
1 cup water
2 ½ tablespoons unsweetened
cocoa powder
½ vanilla bean, split (optional)

Serves 1
Preparation: 10 minutes

Chocolat frappé

Chocolate Milkshake

2 scoops chocolate ice cream
(see page 150)
or sorbet (see page 156)
3/4 cup hot chocolate, cooled
(see page 159)
1 tablespoon heavy cream

1. Place the ice cream or sorbet in a blender, add the cooled chocolate milk and blend for 2 minutes. Add the heavy cream and blend for 30 seconds more.
2. Pour into a tall drinking glass and serve immediately.

Tip: Serve decorated with whipped cream and grated or shaved chocolate.

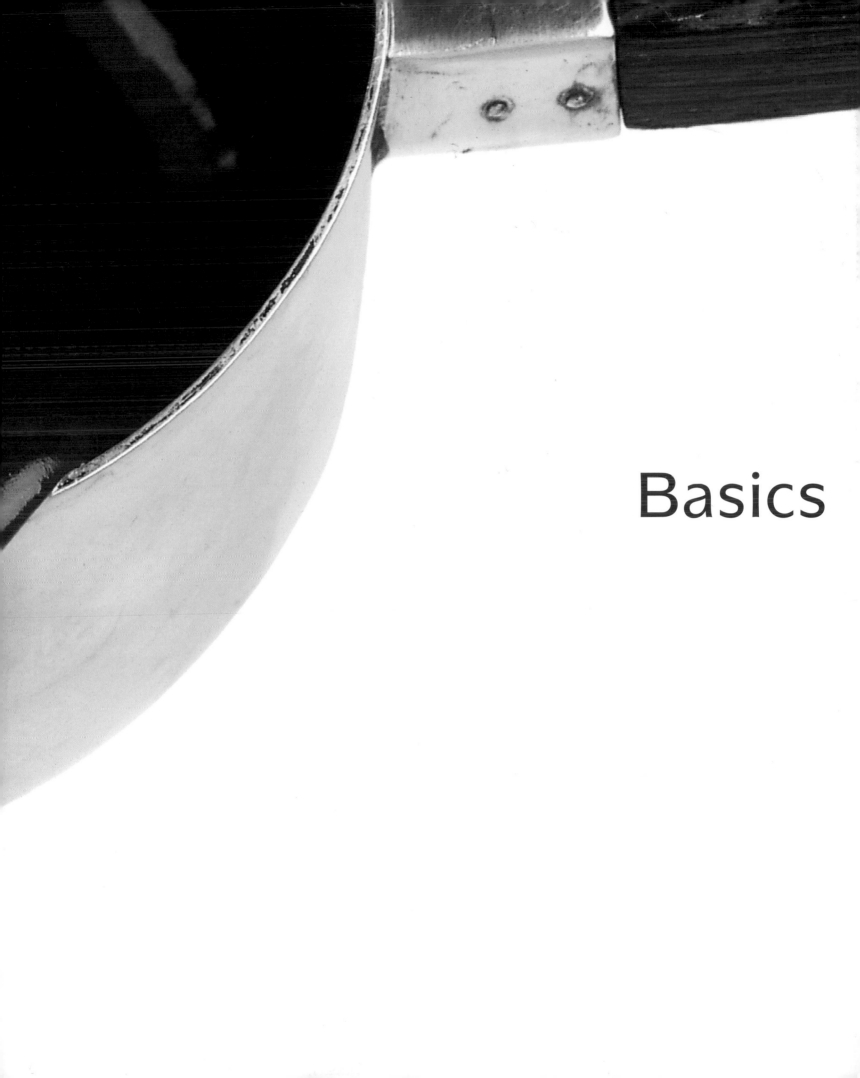

Basics

Ganache

Tempering Chocolate

Basic filling for cakes and chocolates

1. Place the cream in a saucepan and bring to a boil. Meanwhile, finely chop the chocolate and place in a heatproof bowl.

2. Pour the boiling cream over the chocolate and let rest, untouched, for 30 seconds. Slowly begin whisking, starting from the center and working out, until the chocolate is completely melted.

Basic method for making a chocolate coating for cookies, small pastries, and chocolates

1. Finely chop the chocolate and place two-thirds in the top of a double boiler to melt. Stir occasionally. Remove from the heat just before it is completely melted. Add the remaining chopped chocolate in small batches, mixing well after each addition, until completely melted.

2. When the last traces of chocolate have melted, prepare a small sheet of parchment paper. Spoon on a small blob of chocolate: if it hardens in a few minutes, the chocolate is at the correct temperature for proceeding with your recipe. If it takes longer, leave the chocolate until cooler. On the other hand, if the chocolate hardens too quickly, gently reheat by placing on top of a double boiler for a few seconds.

Tip: Another temperature test is to dip a wooden spatula into the melted chocolate and bring it to your upper lip: it should feel cold but fluid.

Chocolate Glaze

Basic recipe for glazing cakes and pastries

1 ²/₃ cup whole milk

14 ¹/₂ ounces bittersweet chocolate

(10 ounces maracaïbo,

4 ¹/₂ ounces ordinary)

1 ounce glucose

2 tablespoons unsalted butter

Place the milk in a saucepan and bring to a boil. Meanwhile, finely chop the chocolate and place in a heatproof bowl. Pour the boiling milk over the chocolate and stir gently to blend; do not beat. Add the glucose and butter, and stir until the mixture is smooth and glossy.

Cover the bowl with plastic wrap and refrigerate until needed. You may use the glaze immediately while it is still lukewarm and fluid, or use in small quantities as needed. If preparing in advance, reheat to soften in the top of a double boiler before using.

This glaze will keep, covered, up to 1 week in the refrigerator.

Tip: Stir the glaze very gently to avoid adding air bubbles to the mixture.

Chopped Chocolate

Place the chocolate on a chopping board and chop finely with a knife. The smaller the pieces, the quicker the chocolate will melt.

Infusing with Mint

To flavor a ganache, warm the cream and add fresh mint leaves (or another fresh herb). Remove from the heat and let infuse. Strain to remove the leaves before pouring the cream on the chocolate.

Melting Chocolate

Place the chopped chocolate in the top of a double boiler and melt over low heat, stirring occasionally. Avoid getting water into the mixture as this will cause it to thicken.

Glazing a Cake

To coat a cake with chocolate, melt the chocolate or the ganache. As soon as it is smooth and liquid, pour on top of the cake, spreading evenly with a thin palette knife. Set aside to harden.

To add texture

For a rippled effect, glaze the cake with chocolate and let stand for about 2 minutes. Using a ridged spreading tool, create a wavy pattern. Let harden without touching.

Chocolate Shavings

Prepare chocolate for tempering (see page 164). As soon as the chocolate melts, pour onto a large, smooth cold surface (a marble board is ideal). Spread very thinly and, just before it cools completely, scrape the surface with the blade of a knife to obtain shavings.

Chocolate Leaves

To make a chocolate leaf decoration, begin with very clean leaves, preferably those that have distinct veins. Prepare chocolate for tempering (see page 164). Using a small pastry brush, cover the textured side of the leaf with melted chocolate. Set aside to harden. As soon as the chocolate hardens, carefully pull away the real leaf.

To cut perfect slices from soft chocolate cakes

Begin with a cake that is well chilled. Choose a knife with a thin blade. Begin by running the blade under hot water, then quickly wipe dry. Cut the cake, wiping the knife clean between each slice. Before serving, let the cake stand at room temperature; it should not be eaten too cold.

Cocoa Tree Pods: These are about 6 inches long and contain up to 40 cocoa beans. A good cocoa tree can produce up to 25 pods per year.

Conversions Chart and Suppliers

Conversions

1 tablespoon: 15ml

¼ cup: 60ml

⅓ cup: 80ml

½ cup: 125ml

1 cup: 250ml

1 quart: 1000ml (1 liter)

1 ounce: 30g

¼ pound: 125g

⅓ pound: 150g

6 ounces: 180g

7 ounces: 200g

½ pound: 250g

10 ounces: 300g

¾ pound 375g

1 pound: 500g

200°F: 100°C

300°F: 150°C

325°F: 170°C

350°F: 180°C

375°F: 190°C

400°F: 200°C

425°F: 220°C

¼ inch: 5mm

½ inch: 1cm

4 inches: 10cm

6 inches: 15cm

8 inches: 20cm

10 inches: 25cm

Suppliers

The following can supply equipment and special ingredients such as sheet gelatin, fondant, couverture chocolate, chestnut purée, etc. Please check with suppliers for availability.

CIA AT GREYSTONE
Phone: 888-424-2433
Fax: 877-967-2433

DEAN & DELUCA
Phone: 800-221-7714
Fax: 212-226-6800
Internet: www.dean-deluca.com

LA MAISON DU CHOCOLAT, USA
1018 Madison Avenue
New York, NY 10021
Phone: 212-744-7117

30 Rockefeller Center
New York, NY 10112
Phone: 212-265-9404
Toll free: 800-988-LMDC / 800-988-5632
Internet: www.lamaisonduchocolat.com

SURFAS
Phone: 310-559-4770